W9-ARG-016

1960: 800 Americans in Vietnam . . .

1966: 400,000 Americans in Vietnam . . .

Vietnam—The border skirmish that has become the fourth largest war in United States history—*the war nobody wanted.*

Other Fawcett Crest Books by
Arthur M. Schlesinger, Jr.

A THOUSAND DAYS

JOHN F. KENNEDY IN THE WHITE HOUSE

ARTHUR M. SCHLESINGER, JR.

THE
BITTER
HERITAGE

VIETNAM AND AMERICAN DEMOCRACY
1941-1966

A FAWCETT CREST BOOK

Fawcett Publications, Inc., Greenwich, Conn.
Member of American Book Publishers Council, Inc.

Acknowledgments

In writing this book I have drawn on three articles—"A Middle Way Out of Vietnam," *New York Times Magazine*, September 18, 1966; "On the Inscrutability of History," *Encounter*, November 1966; and "McCarthyism Is Threatening Us Again," *Saturday Evening Post*, August 13, 1966—as well as on certain passages in *A Thousand Days* (Boston, 1965).

A.M.S., Jr.

A Fawcett Crest Book reprinted by arrangement with Houghton Mifflin Company.
This book contains the complete text of the original hardcover edition.

Library of Congress Catalog Card Number: 67-15978

PRINTING HISTORY
Houghton Mifflin Company edition published January 19, 1967
First printing, December 1966
Second printing, March 1967

First Fawcett Crest printing, May 1967

Published by Fawcett World Library
67 West 44th Street, New York, N. Y. 10036
Printed in the United States of America

For those fighting in Vietnam

As Lord Milner put it some time later on, 'in a certain sense the war would never be ended'; it would just fade away. The guerrilla phase would be ended by the armies; and after that, brigandage in the mountains and the back-veldts would be put down by armed police.

This was an error destined to cost us dear. . . . The flames of partisan warfare broke out again and again in regions completely pacified. . . . This long-drawn struggle bred shocking evils. . . .

Never, never, never believe any war will be smooth and easy. . . . The Statesman who yields to war fever must realize that once the signal is given he is no longer the master of policy but the slave of unforeseeable and uncontrollable events. Antiquated War Offices, weak, incompetent or arrogant Commanders, untrustworthy allies, hostile neutrals, malignant Fortune, ugly surprises, awful miscalculations—all take their seats at the Council Board. . . . Always remember, however sure you are that you can easily win, that there would not be a war if the other man did not think he also had a chance.

—Winston S. Churchill,
A Roving Commission: My Early Life

Contents

Remarks on United States Foreign Policy
by ARTHUR M. SCHLESINGER, JR.
March 8, 1967

*T*HE situation in Vietnam presents us with our most urgent problem today in the field of foreign affairs. But the Vietnam problem is only the most vivid expression of a deeper crisis in American foreign policy. The roots of this deeper crisis lie not in the malevolence of men but in the obsolescence of ideas.

For we live in a time when the velocity of history is greater than ever before. The world has changed more in the last hundred years than it did in the thousand years preceding. The transformations wrought by science and technology have acquired a cumulative momentum and an exponential effect. One consequence is that perceptions of reality become obsolete with new and disconcerting rapidity. This would be all right, if the way we perceive reality changed as reality itself changes. But, as we all know, it doesn't. Our perceptions of reality are crystallized in a collection of stereotypes; and people become so fond of the stereotypes, so much at home with them, that they stop looking at actuality. In this way they protect themselves from the most painful of human necessities, which is, of course, the taking of thought.

The rapidity with which reality outstrips our perceptions of reality is an underlying source of our troubles with foreign policy. I do not suggest that, if our perceptions were kept up to date, this would solve all our problems, because many of the great problems of the world are in their nature insoluble. But I am sure that we cannot make much sense at all in the world as long as we continue to base policy on anachronism. We must be forever vigilant to prevent transient strategies from turning into cherished and permanent verities.

Thus the ideas which dominate our foreign policy today were largely shaped by a very different world— a world threatened by massive, unitary, centralized movements of military aggression and social fanaticism: Adolf Hitler and Nazism in the thirties, Josef Stalin and Communism in the forties and early fifties. These ideas were admirably suited for this world and admirably achieved their objectives. They reflected a great and challenging time in world history, and the men who grew up in that time and acquired those ideas quite naturally find it hard to relinquish them. Yet the world itself has changed drastically—and this fact surely demands the review, if not the revision, of the presuppositions of our policy.

The most drastic change of all has taken place, as this essay points out, within the Communist empire itself. Twenty years ago Communism was still relatively monolithic in ideology and in discipline. Communist parties and governments everywhere took their orders from Moscow. A new Communist state meant the automatic extension of Russian national power; and, given the character of Soviet purpose, this in turn meant an increased threat to the security and freedom of the democracies. Communism, in short, was a unified and expanding international movement capable of the gravest possible challenge to the democratic world.

But that was 1947. It was true through the years of the Korean War. But it is now 1967, and Communism today is in a very different situation. For the quarrel between Moscow and Peking means the irrevocable end of the unity of Communist discipline and ideology. It means the disappearance of any sole and single center of authority in the Communist empire. It has consequently set all Communist states free to respond to national interests and to pursue national policies. It has thereby transformed the character of the Communist problem. In this new polycentrist world, divergent nationalist forces are producing a wide diversity of behavior among the Communist states. Communism is no longer a unified, coordinated, centralized world conspiracy. This is the new reality which wise policy must surely begin to take into account.

The administration has partly recognized this evolution of affairs so far as Eastern Europe is concerned. President Johnson's emphasis on "bridge-building," as in his excellent speech last October, expresses a shrewd understanding of the advantages to the United States in encouraging diversity within the European Communist bloc and in enlarging the ties between the Eastern European states and the West. But we have not yet begun to apply this understanding to the problems of Western Europe. For in Western Europe we still seem committed to policies which were superbly brave and right in the world of twenty years ago but are much less germane to the world today.

So long as we insist on regarding NATO, for example, as first of all a means of deterring a Soviet invasion of Western Europe, we doom it to irrelevance. Thus the Chairman of the Joint Chiefs of Staff said only the other day, "The threat is, if anything, greater than it was in the day [our troops] were put there." If this assertion represents the administration's perception of European reality, one can only admire so stern and determined a fidelity to the truths of yesteryear. For, whatever the danger twenty years ago when Western Europe was politically demoralized and economically prostrate, the notion that an invasion of Western Europe ranks very high on Moscow's list of priorities today obviously requires an extraordinary *tour de force* of the imagination.

And, in the Far East, the administration seems determined to perceive Communism as it was a generation ago. It evidently regards East Asian Communism as a homogeneous and disciplined movement of international aggression, posing a threat to the United States comparable to that posed by Hitler in the thirties or Stalin in the forties. "The contest in Vietnam," the President has said, "is part of a wider pattern of aggressive purposes." The Secretary of State's constant reliance on the Munich analogy makes it clear that he sees the United States as challenged, not by ragged bands of guerrillas in black pajamas without heavy artillery or air power, but by a heavily armed, highly wound-up, overwhelmingly strong military power committed to the course of instant expansion.

For the evidence fails to sustain the thesis that the war in Vietnam is Mao's war or that the Viet Cong are only the spearhead of a Chinese program of aggression. Indeed, most of the evidence suggests that Asian Communism is as fragmented as—perhaps even more fragmented than—European Communism. The proposition that we are fighting in Asia to restrain Chinese aggression —that we must fight in Vietnam today or else we will be fighting in Hawaii tomorrow—is a product not of contemporary evidence but of mechanical historical analogy. It represents the triumph of stereotype over reality. For the evidence strongly suggests that we confront in Vietnam, not a fateful tests of wills with China, but a nasty local war, mounted by Communists who want to take over Vietnam, not for Peking but for themselves— and who, if they succeeded, might be no more enslaved by Peking than North Korea is today.

This is, of course, a very different situation from the one described to us by the administration. It is a more manageable situation—and also a situation calling far less for the sacrifice of American lives. And, if this is the real situation, the argument for bringing the war to an end and stopping the killing seems very strong indeed. Hence the great present concern with the problem of negotiation.

One can have no question about the genuineness of President Johnson's wish for a negotiated settlement in Vietnam. But the administration has made it clear, I would judge, that, while negotiation remains its ultimate objective, it does not consider negotiation advantageous at this time (April 1967). Why else, unless it thought this, would Washington have hardened the American terms at the very time that Hanoi apparently allowed Moscow to soften the North Vietnamese terms?

In April 1965 Hanoi laid down its Four Points as a basis for negotiation. These points were not very helpful. They included such hopeless stipulations as the withdrawal of United States forces from South Vietnam (though it was not always clear whether this meant withdrawal in advance of negotiations) and the final settlement of the internal affairs of South Vietnam "in accordance with the program" of the Viet Cong. These points, especially if the first implied prior withdrawal, were clearly and rightly unacceptable to the United States.

The American position as it evolved in response was that the United States was prepared to suspend the bombing of North Vietnam for "nothing more," as *Time* magazine has put it, "than an agreement to begin negotiations." Thus the Secretary of State said on February 16, 1966, "Some governments said Hanoi would talk if we would stop bombing North Vietnam. We tried that twice . . . but it made no difference. Hanoi would not come to the conference table." On March 13, 1966, the Vice President said that, if Hanoi had shown any interest in negotiation during the recent bombing pause, this "obviously would have kept the bombing pause going."

Now, a year later, both Kosygin and U Thant said that North Vietnam was prepared to meet these terms. If the United States unconditionally stopped the bombing of North Vietnam, these authorities claimed, negotiation could begin. There was no mention of the Four Points. In other words, as Mr. Lippmann has put it, they "brought us the assurance that our 1966 terms—suspension for an unconditional parley—would now be accepted by Hanoi." One cannot be sure, of course, that Moscow could have delivered Hanoi to the conference table on these terms. Ho Chi Minh's passion for negotiation is, to put it mildly, reserved and equivocal; and his tone is abominable. But this is no argument against making the attempt. The whole Soviet initiative was unprecedented, and, if it had been taken up, the responsibility for producing Hanoi would have fallen on Moscow. If we really wanted negotiation, we had a good chance of having it in 1967 on the same terms that we sought it in 1966.

But these terms were evidently now unacceptable to us. For Washington has considerably stiffened its position and now demands from Hanoi things it did not demand a year ago. Publicly we have only asked for the prior assurance of some unspecified act of reciprocal de-escalation—"just almost any step," the President said—in return for the cessation of the bombing. But privately President Johnson in his letter of February 2 to Ho Chi Minh was far more specific and drastic. He then said he would stop the bombing of North Vietnam only "as soon as I am assured that infiltration into South Vietnam by land and by sea has been stopped." This meant, in the view of Mr. Reston of *The New York Times*, "that the North Vietnamese [had to] act *first* to stop the infiltration . . . before the United States stops the bombing." It meant that Ho Chi Minh could no longer supply his forces in South Vietnam while the United States retained the right to supply American forces. President Johnson's offer to desist at the same time from "further augmentation of United States forces in South Vietnam" could hardly have been deeply moving to those in Hanoi who reflected that there were already 420,000 American troops in South Vietnam as against 50,000 Vietnamese regulars and that, under the President's terms, the American troops would be free, in the words of Mr. Reston, "to hunt and destroy an enemy cut off from his supplies in the North." Could anyone have honestly supposed that such a proposition would be faintly interesting to Hanoi?

Not only did President Johnson thus harden the American position beyond anything disclosed to the American people (his letter to Ho Chi Minh was released by Hanoi); but he described the North Vietnamese proposal as one requiring that we cease " 'unconditionally' and *permanently* [emphasis added] our bombing operations against your country." The repeated American insistence that Hanoi demands a "permanent" cessation of bombing reinforces the impression of our reluctance to negotiate at this time. For neither Kosygin nor Podgorny said anything about "permanent" cessation. Ho Chi Minh's reply to President Johnson said that "if the U.S. Government really wants these talks, it must first of all stop unconditionally its bombing raids and all other acts of war against the Democratic Republic of Vietnam." He did not use the word *permanent*. The very idea that one state could expect another to pledge never, never, never, in whatever contingency and in all perpetuity, to refrain from bombing another state is self-evidently absurd. It would represent a derogation of sovereignty that no nation would ever accept. No doubt the word "permanent" sounded at some point in the medley of voices out of Hanoi. But a resourceful diplomacy, thus faced with conflicting proposals, would surely have done as we did when confronted by two contradictory proposals from Khrushchev during the Cuban missile crisis: it would have responded to the one that suited our interests best. Had we followed in October 1962 the practice of ignoring the acceptable and fastening on the unacceptable proposal, we might well have stumbled into the Third World War.

If we had really wanted negotiation in February 1967, we would have ended the bombing as the Russians suggested and let the burden of delivering Hanoi to the conference table fall to Moscow. On the other hand, if we could not figure out how negotiation at this point could yield satisfactory results, we would do exactly as we did —ignore the Soviet initiative, claim that we knew Hanoi's mind better than Kosygin and Podgorny did, acknowledge only the most extreme and extravagant proposals from North Vietnam and put forward proposals of our own that we could be absolutely certain Hanoi would not accept. The actions of the administration lead irresistibly to the conclusion that it does not consider this a favorable time to negotiate, and that it cannot summon up the energy or imagination to seek a solution in unfavorable circumstances.

One regrets that high officials have seen fit to accompany this by rather far-fetched misrepresentations of other people's ideas. Thus the Secretary of State said, "Proposals substantially similar to those put forward by Senator Kennedy were explored prior, during, and since the Tet truce—all without result." Yet the Secretary of

State, who is an intelligent man, must surely know that the administration proposal, insisting as it did on prior action by Hanoi, was very different from Senator Kennedy's proposal. How could he possibly describe two proposals—one for the conditional and the other for the unconditional cessation of bombing—as "substantially similar"? And how for that matter could the President of the United States imply that the cessation of the bombing of the north would leave our soldiers defenseless in the south? "If they are going to lob their mortar shells into the backs of our soldiers," he said, ". . . you must, if you are at all fair to those who are defending you there, permit them to respond." I know of no proposals that American troops should stop defending themselves or even any for the cessation of bombing in the south. Such misstatements advance neither the clarity of the debate nor the credibility of the administration.

Still, I do not suggest that the administration's evident desire to postpone negotiations is without rational justification. The reasoning behind it, I imagine, runs something like this. The administration apparently regards the recent signals from Hanoi as a response to the bombing of the north and, in consequence, a vindication of the bombing policy. At the same time, it evidently does not see how, given the present military balance, a negotiation can lead to a desirable outcome. It looks forward, moreover, to the stabilization of the political situation in South Vietnam through the formation of a civilian government (though, if Marshal Ky should end up as head of this government, it seems doubtful how much more stable the situation would be). Therefore, it reasons, if we bomb a few months more, Hanoi will be even more anxious to end the war than it is today; Saigon will be in better shape; and at that point we can negotiate under much more advantageous conditions.

This analysis is not illogical, and it may well be right. But it is not so self-evidently right as to be immune to question. For one thing, its basic assumption is that the peace signals are as a response to bombing. Yet it is entirely possible—I should say, even probable—that the signals from Hanoi are a response, not to our air war in the north, but to our ground war in the south. Hanoi and the Viet Cong may well have come to the conclusion that they can hope neither for a military victory in the south nor an American withdrawal, and that they therefore must begin to shift from the idea of a short-run military victory to that of a long-run political victory. Furthermore, the turmoil in China has doubtless conferred a greater freedom of action on Hanoi. These reasons are quite sufficient to explain Hanoi's renewed interest in negotiations, without supposing that it is all a result of bombing.

Moreover, the theory that we can obtain more favorable terms by intensifying the war is based on an old fallacy—that, while we escalate, the other side will sit still, and that escalation will consequently bring us a clear margin of superiority. This has been the reasoning behind every previous step of escalation; and it has always proved wrong. The other side, instead of sitting still, had escalated too. Instead of achieving a margin of superiority, all we have done is to raise the stalemate to a more bloody and more explosive level. The Russians, for example, cannot be expected to do nothing while we widen the war in North Vietnam. They are already increasing their shipments of anti-aircraft missiles and guns and other arms and supplies. Our bombing will further harden the resolve of the North Vietnamese themselves. If past experience has any relevance, the consequence in six months of this new exercise in escalation will be, not at all the victory the generals keep promising us, but a new and even more perilous stalemate.

The problem is that there is never a right time for negotiation. In the past some in Hanoi have no doubt construed our own calls for negotiation as a sign of weakness and have, in consequence, argued for stiffening their own position. So some in Washington today construe Hanoi's signals as a sign of weakness, contend that the enemy is on the run and call for an intensification of military pressure. By this logic we cannot negotiate when we are behind because we are weak; and we can't negotiate either when we are ahead because, if we keep on doing what we have been doing, we will be even farther ahead at some later point.

The time has surely come to break the hopeless logic which can never find the right moment for negotiation. Too much is imperiled by the continuation of the war: the lives of American soldiers, as well as of the Vietnamese; the confidence and support of our allies; our position in Europe and Latin America; our relationship with the Soviet Union; not to mention the vast needs of our national society—our cities, our schools, our poor, our minorities, our old and our young.

The urgent need is to explore every opportunity to slow down the war. The bombing of North Vietnam has failed to halt the infiltration or to break the will of the people of North Vietnam or to bring Hanoi to the conference table. Moreover, if we bombed North Vietnam back to the stone age tomorrow, the war would continue in South Vietnam. The cruel fact is that we can never win a guerrilla war in South Vietnam by the aerial obliteration of North Vietnam. Instead, therefore, of seeking excuses to avoid negotiation, instead of upping our ante and insisting on the worst possible interpretations of our adversaries' position, it would be interesting for us to appear for a moment before the world as the champion, not of bombing and destruction, but of vision and peace.

There is a deeper question involved here—and that has to do with the character of America's role in the world. There is abroad in the land the notion that foreign policy is not, as we have traditionally supposed, about the accommodation of conflicting national entities, but about questions of right and wrong. This, oddly enough, is a view of foreign policy shared by the Secretary of State and the New Left. And one detects in some of our official pronouncements the implication that the United States, as a result of its inherent moral superiority, is the world's judge, jury and executioner; and that, where things are wrong, it is the American mission to set them right. This seems a distorted, even dangerous, view of the American role in the world. For, while the men who founded this republic did believe that America had a mission to mankind, they conceived this mission as one to be spread by example and persuasion, not by force. John Quincy Adams well stated the classical American creed when he noted that the United States would always view with sympathy any foreign group struggling for independence: "But she goes not abroad in search of monsters to destroy. She is the well-wisher to the freedom and independence of all. She is the champion and vindicator only of her own."

I fear a current tendency to go abroad in search of monsters to destroy. Yet this enterprise ignores the limitations on our own knowledge and on our own power. President Kennedy put the matter well some years ago: "We must face the fact that the United States is neither omnipotent nor omniscient—that we are only 6 per cent of the world's population—that we cannot impose our will on the other 94 per cent of mankind— that we cannot right every wrong or reverse each adversary—and that therefore there cannot be an American solution to every world problem."

The world is filled with contradiction and evil and will continue to be so for a long time. We cannot hope to resolve every contradiction and overcome all the evils and produce an American solution to every problem—especially if we try to do so on the basis of stereotypes which express the reality of another generation. It is bad enough to be a messiah; it is even worse to be a messiah spouting clichés. And, if we insist on casting ourselves as the world's savior, the effect on ourselves will be as fatal as on the rest of mankind. For no one can play God with impunity. "He who would act the angel," said Pascal, "acts the brute"—a warning alike to men and nations.

I

HOW WE GOT THERE

*W*HY we are in Vietnam is today a question of mainly historical interest. We *are* there, for better or for worse, and we must deal with the situation that exists. Our national security may not have compelled us to draw a line across Southeast Asia where we did, but, having drawn it, we cannot lightly abandon it. Our stake in South Vietnam may have been self-created, but it has none the less become real. Our precipitate withdrawal now would have ominous reverberations throughout Asia. The magnitude of our national concern is measured by our commitment of over 400,000 troops, young men of exceptional skill and gallantry, engaged in cruel and difficult warfare. This is a larger force than we had in Korea fifteen years ago—larger indeed than we have had in any war in our history, except for the Civil War and the two World Wars. More American soldiers already have died in combat in Vietnam than in the Revolutionary War, the War of 1812, the Mexican War or the Spanish-American War.

We must, I say, deal with the situation that exists. We cannot undo the events which have brought us to this tragic climax. Still, a glance at the past may at least remind us of illusions which will otherwise continue to mislead us in the future. For our experience with Vietnam is older than we generally recognize. This is not the first time, for example, that Vietnam has involved us in war. In 1941 Franklin Roosevelt regarded the Japanese movement into Indochina as a threat to vital American interests. He saw it as a threat because the occupation of Vietnam would give Japan a base for larger aggression against all Southeast Asia and also, more specifically, because it would jeopardize the supply of natural rubber upon which the American defense industry depended. In consequence, the Japanese demands on Indochina in July 1941 led directly to the American decision to freeze Japanese assets in the United States; and this action, in turn, led directly to the Japanese decision to attack the American fleet at Pearl Harbor.

Vietnam thus precipitated American entry into the Second World War; nor did this faraway land thereafter disappear from the mind of the American President. Convinced that the war would set off a world-wide revolt against European colonialism, Roosevelt judged Indochina one of the weakest links in the chain of western empire. In March 1943 he therefore proposed to the British Foreign Minister, Anthony Eden, that Indochina, instead of being restored to the French after the war, should be placed under an international trusteeship and prepared for independence. He discussed this idea with Chiang Kai-shek at the Cairo Conference and with Stalin at Teheran. When the State Department suggested to the President in early 1944 that the French army would undoubtedly return to Indochina in the natural course of military events, Roosevelt told Under Secretary Stettinius that "no French troops whatever should be used in operations in Indo-China." He told Secretary Hull: "France has had the country—thirty million inhabitants—for nearly one hundred years, and the people are worse off than they were at the beginning. . . . France has milked it for one hundred years. The people of Indochina are entitled to something better

than that." Indochina was much on his mind when he
went to Yalta in February 1945. "For two whole years,"
he then said—

> I have been terribly worried about Indochina. . . . I
> suggested . . . to Chiang, that Indochina be set up
> under a trusteeship—have a Frenchman, one or two
> Indochinese, and a Chinese and a Russian, because
> they are on the coast, and maybe a Filipino and an
> American, to educate them for self-government. . . .
>   Stalin liked the idea, China liked the idea. The Brit-
> ish didn't like it. It might bust up their empire, because
> if the Indochinese were to work together and eventu-
> ally get their independence, the Burmese might do the
> same thing.

Roosevelt's proposal had a certain eccentricity of
detail; but it was founded in realism and wisdom, and,
if its essence had been carried out, the world might have
been spared much bloodshed and agony. Alas, the idea
died with him a few months later. The State Department soon expressed the belief that there could be no
trusteeship in Indochina "except under the French
Government," adding vaguely that it was President Truman's purpose "at some appropriate time" to ask France
for "some positive indication of its intention in regard
to the establishment of basic liberties and an increasing
measure of self-government in Indochina."

Five months after Roosevelt's death, Ho Chi Minh,
a Vietnamese Communist who had served the Comin-
tern for twenty years and had more recently emerged
as a leader of the anti-Japanese resistance movement
(in which capacity he had worked closely with the
American Office of Strategic Services), proclaimed the
Declaration of Independence of the Democratic Republic of Vietnam. This document, curiously, was modeled
on the American Declaration of 1776 and actually began with the exceedingly non-Marxist quotation: "All
men are created equal. They are endowed by their
Creator with certain unalienable rights, among these are

Life, Liberty and the pursuit of Happiness." The French responded by a determined attempt to re-establish colonial rule. For the next eight years this effort, occasionally interrupted by spasms of negotiation, brought the French and such Vietnamese as they could persuade to go along with them into increasingly savage conflict with the Viet Minh under Ho Chi Minh—who, in consequence, emerged increasingly as the hero of Vietnamese nationalism in its war for independence.

The American government at first paid little attention to the fighting in Vietnam. But the fall of mainland China to the Chinese Communists in 1949 and the invasion of South Korea by the North Korean Communists in 1950 produced new anxieties about communist expansion in Asia. In this light the French appeared to be holding the southern line against Asian communism; the State Department, condemning Ho as "an agent of world communism," pronounced the French role in Indochina "an integral part of the worldwide resistance by the Free Nations to Communist attempts at conquest and subversion"; and, once the Paris government had satisfied the American anti-colonial conscience by making token concessions to its client regime in Saigon under Emperor Bao Dai, the Truman administration was prepared to send the French military and economic equipment. The Eisenhower administration enlarged this policy. By 1954, according to French figures, the United States was paying 78.25 per cent (490 billion old francs) of the French cost of the war; the French were paying 21.75 per cent (136 billion old francs).

Our growing involvement in Indochina was taking place for reasons less specific than those which had moved Roosevelt a dozen years earlier. The wartime development of synthetic rubber had long since ended American dependence on Asian rubber plantations. Nor did an internal revolt of a band of Vietnamese nationalists, even if led by Communists, threaten all Southeast Asia as had the external conquest of the country a decade before by a powerful militarist state dedicated to the establishment of the Greater East Asia Co-prosperity Sphere. Secretary of State Dulles tried to supply this deficiency by invoking the specter of China. "There is a risk," he said in September 1953, "that, as in Korea, Red China might send its own army into Indochina. The Chinese Communist regime should realize that such a second aggression could not occur without grave consequences, which might not be confined to Indochina." But the prospect of a Viet Minh victory even without Chinese intervention was soon deemed almost as alarming. "You have a row of dominoes set up," President Eisenhower explained at a press conference early in 1954, "you knock over the first one, and what will happen to the last one is that it will go over very quickly." So the domino theory entered the political vocabulary. Even though the biggest domino of all, China, had fallen five years earlier without starting the chain reaction, the possible fall of the less consequential Indochinese domino was suddenly invested with the most fateful consequences.

The commander of the French force beleaguered in the fortress of Dien Bien Phu now began to plead for American military relief. Within the American government Admiral Radford, then chairman of the Joint Chiefs of Staff, proposed an air strike from the Philippines. A few days later Vice President Nixon even suggested the possibility of "putting our boys in." However, President Eisenhower, doubtful about unilateral military intervention, decided to seek British collaboration. "If . . . Indochina passes into the hands of the Communists," he wrote Prime Minister Winston Churchill on April 4, 1954, "the ultimate effect on our and your global strategic position . . . could be disastrous. . . . We failed to halt Hirohito, Mussolini and Hitler by not acting in unity and in time. That marked the beginning of many years of stark tragedy and desperate peril. May it not be that our nations have learned something from that lesson?" Then Dulles pressed on Anthony

Eden, once again Foreign Secretary, the case for joint intervention. "I am fairly hardened to crises," Eden wrote later, "but I went to bed that night a troubled man. I did not believe that anything less than intervention on a Korean scale, if that, would have any effect in Indochina." Churchill thus summed up the American proposal: "What we are being asked to do is to assist in misleading the Congress into approving a military operation which would be in itself ineffective, and might well bring the world to the verge of a major war."

The campaign for intervention also caused concern in Washington. The Army Chief of Staff, General Matthew B. Ridgway, who had commanded the United Nations army in Korea, and the Chief of Plans, General James M. Gavin, both questioned the theory that bombing could reverse the tide of war, and both regarded the commitment of the American Army to war on the Asian mainland as strategically indefensible. "In Korea," as Ridgway later wrote, "we had learned that air and naval power alone cannot win a war and that inadequate ground forces cannot win one either. It was incredible to me that we had forgotten that bitter lesson so soon—that we were on the verge of making that same tragic error."

And in the United States Congress a number of senators expressed their doubts about the direction of American policy. Senator John F. Kennedy of Massachusetts had visited Indochina in 1951. "We have allied ourselves," he had said on his return, "to the desperate effort of a French regime to hang on to the remnants of empire. . . . To check the southern drive of communism makes sense but not only through reliance on the force of arms. The task is rather to build a strong native non-communist sentiment within these areas and rely on that as a spearhead of defense rather than upon the legions of General de Lattre. To do this apart from and in defiance of innately nationalistic aims spells foredoomed failure. . . . Without the support of the native population, there is no hope of success in any of the countries of Southeast Asia."

Now Kennedy rose in the Senate to say that, if the American people were to go to war for the fourth time in the century, "particularly a war which we now realize would threaten the survival of civilization," they had a right to inquire in detail into the nature of the struggle and the possible alternatives. He recapitulated the Washington litany about Indochina—Secretary of State Dean Acheson in 1952 ("the military situation appears to be developing favorably"), Assistant Secretary of State for the Far East Walter Robertson in 1953 ("in Indochina we believe the tide is now turning"), Secretary of Defense Charles Wilson (French victory is "both possible and probable") and Admiral Radford ("the French are going to win") in 1954—and contrasted the gush of official optimism with the grim actuality. "I am frankly of the belief," Kennedy said, "that no amount of American military assistance in Indochina can conquer . . . 'an enemy of the people' which has the sympathy and covert support of the people. . . . For the United States to intervene unilaterally and to send troops into the most difficult terrain in the world, with the Chinese able to pour in unlimited manpower, would mean that we would face a situation whch would be far more difficult than even that we encountered in Korea. It seems to me it would be a hopeless situation." He asked serious consideration of the question "whether all or part of Indochina is absolutely essential to the security of Asia and the free world."

The Democratic leader in the Senate, Lyndon B. Johnson of Texas, was even harsher about the Eisenhower policy. "The United States," Johnson said,

is in clear danger of being left naked and alone in a hostile world. . . . American foreign policy has never in its history suffered such a stunning reversal. . . . What is American policy on Indochina? All of us have listened to the dismal series of reversals and confusions and alarms and excursions which have emerged from Washington over the past few weeks. . . . We have been caught bluffing by our enemies. Our friends and allies are frightened and wondering, as we do, where we are headed. . . . This picture of our country needlessly weakened in the world today is so painful that we should turn our eyes from abroad and look homeward.

The Eisenhower administration had not hit upon the latter-day doctrine that no one should criticize American policy in Vietnam lest such criticism encourage the enemy—the doctrine by which President Johnson a dozen years later sought to deter the Senator Johnsons of his own day; and the nervous Nellies of 1954 had their effect. The opposition of the congressional leaders, of Generals Ridgway and Gavin and of the British eventually forced the administration to drop the plan of military intervention. Could this plan have worked? Obviously air strikes alone would not have defeated the Viet Minh, and the Army was unquestionably right in supposing that intervention would soon have meant ground forces. If American combat troops had entered Vietnam in 1954 instead of 1965, they could certainly have beaten the Viet Minh in pitched battle; but they could hardly have crushed the guerrilla uprising or the nationalist emotions which sustained it. In retrospect, intervention in 1954 would only have dragged the United States into a conflict which would have seemed to most of Indochina—and most of Asia—a war not against communism but against national independence, a war not for freedom but for France.

But Eisenhower eventually decided against intervention, the French abandoned the fight after the surrender of Dien Bien Phu and negotiations in Geneva, in which the United States declined to take part, resulted in the *de facto* partition of Vietnam at the 17th parallel and the independence of Laos and Cambodia. Two months after Geneva, Dulles, in a conference at Manila, organized the Southeast Asia Treaty Organization (SEATO) including Pakistan, Thailand, the Philippines, Australia, New Zealand, France and Great Britain as well as the United States. A special protocol added South Vietnam, Laos and Cambodia to the area to be protected by the new organization. A few weeks later, Eisenhower, in response to a request from Prime Minister Ngo Dinh Diem of South Vietnam for "economic assistance," pledged American support "to assist the Government of Viet-Nam in developing and maintaining a strong, viable state, capable of resisting attempted subversion or aggression through military means." The United States, Eisenhower continued, expected that this aid would be met "by performance on the part of the Government of Viet-Nam in undertaking needed reforms."

In subsequent years both the SEATO treaty and the 1954 Eisenhower letter to Diem have been cited as not only justifying but *requiring* every action the United States has taken since in Vietnam, including sending in several hundred thousand combat troops eleven years later. Thus during the Senate Foreign Relations Committee hearings on Vietnam in January 1966, Senator Fulbright asked, "Does the Southeast Treaty, Southeast Asia Treaty Organization, commit us to do what we are now doing in Vietnam?" and the Secretary of State replied, "Yes, sir, I have no doubt that it does."

But the proposition that SEATO makes American military intervention mandatory in case of armed attack on South Vietnam finds no warrant in the treaty itself or its legislative history; even the Secretary of State did not advance this audacious idea until January 1966, and, according to Senator Morse, he had twice previously told the Foreign Relations Committee in executive session "that we were not acting in Vietnam under SEATO."[1] In the original SEATO hearings in Novem-

---

[1] The transcript of the hearings of August 6, 1964, before the Senate Foreign Relations Committee, belatedly released in November 1966, discloses that the Secretary of State then testified: "We are not acting specifically under the SEATO Treaty."

ber 1954, Secretary Dulles assured the Senate Foreign Relations Committee that, "if there is a revolutionary movement in Vietnam or in Thailand, we would consult together as to what to do about it . . . but we have no undertaking to put it down; all we have is an undertaking to consult." He added that "the agreement of each of the parties to act to meet the common danger 'in accordance with its constitutional processes' leaves to the judgment of each country the type of action to be taken in the event an armed attack occurs." In the Senate debate on the treaty, Senator H. Alexander Smith, who had been a delegate to the Manila conference, explicitly dismissed the view that the treaty was "a compulsory arrangement for our military participation in case of any attack," adding, "We have no purpose of following any such policy as that of having our forces involved in a ground war. . . . We are not committed to the principle of NATO, namely, that an attack on one is an attack on all, calling for immediate military action without further consideration by Congress." No president of the United States before President Johnson interpreted the SEATO treaty as *compelling* American military intervention, and no other signatory so interprets the treaty today. In short, the Secretary of State's proposition that SEATO *commits* the United States to military intervention can only be regarded as an exercise in historical and legal distortion. Similarly the Eisenhower letter to Diem, as President Eisenhower pointed out himself on August 17, 1965, contemplated only economic and political support for the Saigon government. It was not a warrant for military intervention; indeed, at the end of his presidency, fewer than eight hundred American military personnel were stationed in South Vietnam.

On the other hand, the Eisenhower letter and, to a lesser degree, the special protocol to the SEATO treaty, did draw a line across Southeast Asia. Though these documents did not in any legal way compel American military intervention in South Vietnam, they did in a political way involve the United States in holding that line. That line could have been drawn elsewhere—along the Mekong River, for example, and the northern border of Thailand. No vital strategic interest required that it be drawn where it was.[2] But it *was* drawn in South Vietnam, for better or worse; a vital American interest was thus created where none had existed before; and a series of decisions followed in train which ended by carrying the United States into the fourth largest war of its history.

[2] This was recognized by the Eisenhower administration at the time. Thus in Secretary of State Dulles's press conference on May 11, 1954:

"Q: Do you think, Mr. Secretary, that the Southeast Asia area can be held without Indochina?

Mr. Dulles: I do."

II

WHAT WE DID THERE

THE OBJECT of American policy in South Vietnam, as Eisenhower had written Diem, was to "discourage any who might wish to impose a foreign ideology on your free people." It was not clear that the people were so free or the ideology so foreign as Eisenhower supposed, but his language defined the mood in which Washington began the Vietnam adventure. That mood was essentially moralistic. The commitment to South Vietnam, like the parallel attempt to make the languid country of Laos a bastion of western power, followed directly from the Dulles conception of the world as irrevocably split into two unified and hostile blocs. In such a world, the threat of communism was indivisible,[1] the obligation to oppose that threat un-

---

[1] In fairness to Eisenhower and Dulles, it must be said that most public men of the day shared this theory of the homogeneity of communist power—and, of course, communism was much more homogeneous then than later. The one conspicuous exception was that premature polycentrist General Douglas MacArthur who, in the hearings after his dismissal in 1951, described Moscow as only "one of the loci" of the communist conspiracy and added, "The degree of control and influence that the Kremlin may have in China is quite problematical." This

limited (up to the point, at least, of military action) and any yearning for neutrality in the struggle, in Dulles's word, "immoral."

For this reason, Washington supported Saigon in its determination to ignore the provision in the Geneva Agreements for all-Vietnam elections in 1956. However, the question of the 1956 election was agitated in later years far beyond its importance. For, even if President Eisenhower in his memoirs was ready to concede Ho Chi Minh 80 per cent of the vote, Ho himself never displayed any interest in permitting free elections on *his* side of the 17th parallel. So the *de facto* partition lengthened into a political division, and the Saigon and Hanoi governments both set to work to build the strength of their respective states.

On the other side of the parallel, the United States went ahead on the assumption that economic and political support alone would be sufficient to assure the survival of South Vietnam as an independent state. This was by no means an unreasonable judgment at the time. Few of those later critical of Eisenhower's letter to Diem opposed economic aid to South Vietnam in 1954. In the next five years Washington sent in $2.3 billion of aid—three-fifths economic, the rest military. For a time the policy seemed to be working: rice and sugar production rose; so did textile production; school rooms and medical dispensaries were built; there was a token land reform program; and American advisers helped create a South Vietnamese army.

Under the surface, however, things were less idyllic. All too little of the economic assistance went to the

view differed sharply from the contemporary description of China by Assistant Secretary of State Dean Rusk (May 18, 1951): "The Peiping regime may be a colonial Russian government—a Slavic Manchukuo on a larger scale. It is not the government of China. It does not pass the first test. It is not Chinese." MacArthur's insight, however, was evidently employed to sustain the argument that it would be possible to attack China without provoking a Russian reaction. It did not inform MacArthur's general views of communism.

countryside, where most of the South Vietnamese lived. Our military assistance concentrated on building an army organized, not to fight guerrillas, but to repel a formal, Korean-style invasion from across the northern border. And the stipulation in Eisenhower's 1954 letter conditioning aid on the performance of "needed reforms" was largely forgotten. While American insistence did produce a little in the way of land reform (at least on paper), Ngo Dinh Diem was in the main able to pursue authoritarian political objectives without effective, or even visible, American objection.

Diem represented the older generation of Vietnamese nationalists—upper class, French speaking, Catholic. He had fought long and honorably for national independence, but he was not interested in disturbing the hierarchical structure of classical Vietnamese society. He subdued the religious sects, cleaned up Saigon, sought to restore the ancient Annamese morality and showed himself a man of rectitude and will, devoted and incorruptible. But he could hardly have had less sympathy with the popular aspirations for self-government stirred by the struggle for independence. A profound traditionalist, he considered it the obligation of the masses to respect and obey their leaders. He operated a family despotism in the oriental manner, abolishing elected village government in 1956, centering power in his own hands and those of his brothers, treating opposition as disloyalty and scorning the values and institutions of western democracy. "If we open the window," his sister-in-law, the lovely and serpentine Madame Nhu, once said, "not only sunlight but many bad things will fly in."

So the window was kept tightly shut. Diem's authoritarianism, which increasingly involved manhunts, political reeducation camps and the "regroupment" of population, caused spreading discontent and then armed resistance on the countryside. It is not easy to disentangle the events of these murky years; but few scholars believe that the growing resistance was at the start organized or directed by Hanoi. Indeed, there is some indication that the Communists at first hung back, evidently regarding the South Vietnamese guerrillas— soon to be called the Viet Cong—as putschists and infantile leftists (precisely as the Cuban Communist Party regarded Fidel Castro and the 26th of July movement at the same time in Cuba). The civil insurrection in South Vietnam began to gather force by 1958; it was not until September 1960 that the Communist Party of North Vietnam bestowed its formal blessing and called for the liberation of the south from American imperialism. Ho Chi Minh was now supplying the Viet Cong with training, equipment, strategic advice and even men—perhaps two thousand a year by 1960.[2] Nearly all the guerrillas who came from North Vietnam until we started bombing the north in 1965, however, were South Vietnamese who had gone north in 1954; most of the Viet Cong in any case continued to be recruited in South Vietnam; and most Viet Cong arms and equipment were captured from Diem's army.[3]

The Viet Cong unquestionably expressed a strain of genuine, if fanatic, idealism. They sang:

> We are peasants in soldier's clothing
> Waging the struggle for a class oppressed for thousands
>   of years.
> Our suffering is the suffering of the people.

Nationalists fought side by side with Communists. Many whom Diem had denied a role in political life joined the

---

[2] All Vietnamese statistics are unreliable and must be regarded with inflexible mistrust. See below, Chapter V.

[3] The Pentagon informed I. F. Stone that in the years 1962-1964 the South Vietnamese army lost 27,400 weapons of all sorts to the Viet Cong. During the same period 15,100 weapons were captured from the Viet Cong. The International Control Commission reported only 179 enemy-produced weapons in the eighteen-month period from June 1962 to January 1964. Assuming that half the 15,100 weapons were captured in these eighteen months, one must conclude that the Viet Cong before 1965 fought primarily with captured weapons.

resistance. From 1959 through 1962, according to Douglas Pike, the most careful student of the Viet Cong, the guerrilla effort changed "from a loose, disparate collection of dissident groups, often with nothing more in common than hostility for the Diem government, into a tightly knit movement." And behind this process was a central animating purpose—

> not simply population control but to restructure the social order of the village and train the villagers to control themselves. This was the NLF's one undeviating thrust from the start. Not the killing of ARVN soldiers, not the occupation of real estate, not the preparation for some great pitched battle at an Armageddon or a Dien Bien Phu, but organization in depth of the rural population through the instrument of self-control.[4]

It is important not to become romantic about the Viet Cong. They did not simply represent a movement of rural organization and uplift. They extended their power as much by the fear they incited as by the hope they inspired. And the systematic murder of village headmen—half a dozen a day by 1960—could be an effective weapon, especially when the people of the countryside had been given little reason to prefer the government in Saigon to their own survival. It was warfare in the shadows, ambush and assassination and torture, leaving behind a trail of burned villages, shattered families and weeping women.

By the end of 1960 the guerrilla attacks in Vietnam were increasing in boldness and scope. The success of the Communist guerrillas to the southeast in Laos—the Pathet Lao—had opened up a new corridor of assistance from North Vietnam. The South Vietnamese army, trained by the U.S. Military Assistance Advisory Group to fight quite another sort of war, was ineffective. There

[4] See Douglas Pike, *Vietcong* (Cambridge, 1966). The NLF —National Liberation Front—is the political apparatus of the Viet Cong. ARVN is the Army of the Republic of [South] Vietnam.

were now perhaps 15,000 Viet Cong in South Vietnam, overrunning half the country by day and a good deal more by night. In Saigon opposition grew to Diem, his autocratic methods and his conduct of the war. Discontent centered in the army, where American training, if it had not prepared the young Vietnamese officers for guerrilla warfare, had at least given them a sense of modern methods. In November 1960 a military coup almost overthrew the regime. Diem rode this out. Once back in control, he cracked down on all varieties or potentialities of opposition. He imprisoned or exiled a number of younger officials and, to guard against future coups, began a process of splitting the army and pitting one general against another. Trusting no one, he based himself more and more narrowly on his family, especially on his able and aggressive younger brother, Ngo Dinh Nhu.

In January 1961 the Vietnam mess fell to a new American president. Kennedy, who had long believed that the main communist reliance in the coming period would be on neither nuclear nor conventional but guerrilla war, saw the answer to the Viet Cong insurgency in counter-insurgency. For Kennedy counter-insurgency meant a good deal more than teaching soldiers to black their faces and strangle enemies in the night. Guerrilla warfare, he well understood, was essentially political warfare. Effective counter-insurgency, for example, depended on swift and accurate intelligence from the countryside. The Viet Cong could never be defeated unless the Saigon regime could enlist the support of the peasants. Magsaysay's campaign against the Hukbalahaps in the Philippines suggested the model: tough military action against the enemy, generous provisions for amnesty, real and sweeping social reform.

The first effort of the Kennedy years was to persuade the Diem regime to move along these lines. Success in this effort would have been unlikely in any case, given Diem's conviction that the Americans were impatient, naive and childlike, to be humored but never to be heeded. And it became all the more unlikely when the senior American diplomatic and military officials in Saigon decided that Diem was the key to stability and that the only policy was to win Diem's confidence by assuring him of Washington's unconditional support. Once he believed that Washington was with him, they thought, it might be possible to steer him gently and gradually toward reform, but attempts to bring pressure on Diem, in the view of Ambassador Nolting and General Harkins, would be self-defeating. American newspapermen in Saigon, less moved by the South Vietnamese leader, called this the policy of "sink or swim with Ngo Dinh Diem." Diem and Nhu no doubt swam, but the hope of effective reform sank.

The next question was whether Washington should increase its military assistance. Vice President Lyndon B. Johnson, who visited Saigon in May 1961, reported to Kennedy: "The basic decision in Southeast Asia is here. We must decide whether to help these countries to the best of our ability or throw in the towel and pull back our defenses to San Francisco. . . . More important, we would say to the world in this case that we don't live up to our treaties and don't stand by our friends. This is not my concept. I recommend that we move forward promptly with a major effort to help these countries defend themselves." However, American aid to enable a country to defend itself was—in Johnson's mind in 1961—very different from direct American defense of the country. "American combat troop involvement," he said, "is not only not required, it is not desirable." He went on: "Possibly Americans fail to appreciate fully the subtlety that recently colonial peoples would not look with favor upon governments which invited or accept the return this soon of Western troops. To the extent that fear of ground-troop involvement dominates our political responses to Asia in Congress or elsewhere, it seems most desirable to me to allay those paralyzing fears."

The situation in South Vietnam grew worse over the

summer; and in October 1961 Kennedy sent General Maxwell Taylor and Walt W. Rostow, then (and in 1966 again) a White House aide, on a mission to Saigon. The Taylor-Rostow report recommended an enlargement of the American role, essentially through the penetration of the South Vietnamese army and government by American 'advisers,' attached to Vietnamese military units or government offices and designed to improve the level of local performance. Taylor and Rostow also recommended that an American military task force—perhaps 10,000 men—go to Vietnam, commissioned to conduct combat operations for self-defense and perimeter security and, if the Vietnamese army were hard pressed, to act as an emergency reserve. The report concluded by saying that this program would work only if infiltration from the north were stopped and that therefore, should this infiltration continue, the United States should consider a contingency policy of retaliation against the north, graduated to match the intensity of Hanoi's aid to the Viet Cong.

Kennedy rejected both the northern strategy and the use of combat soldiers. "They want a force of American troops," he remarked privately. "They say it's necessary in order to restore confidence and maintain morale. But it will be just like Berlin. The troops will march in; the bands will play; the crowds will cheer; and in four days everyone will have forgotten. Then we will be told we have to send in more troops. It's like taking a drink. The effect wears off, and you have to take another."

Yet he felt obliged to offer a small drink himself, and he increased the number of military advisers. More drinks were still to come. At the end of 1961, there were 1364 American military personnel in South Vietnam; at the end of 1962, 9865; at the time of Kennedy's death in November 1963, about 15,500. This was the policy of 'one more step'—each new step always promising the success which the previous last step had also promised but had unaccountably failed to deliver. Once, early in the Kennedy administration, the then Chairman of the

Joint Chiefs of Staff outlined to the National Security Council the processes by which each American action in Southeast Asia, if it provoked a communist counteraction, could in turn provoke an even more drastic American response. He concluded, "If we are given the right to use nuclear weapons, we can guarantee victory." Kennedy sat glumly rubbing his upper molar, saying nothing. After a moment someone spoke up: "Mr. President, perhaps you would have the General explain to us what he means by victory." Kennedy grunted and dismissed the meeting. Later he said, "Since he couldn't think of any further escalation, he would have to promise us victory."

With the Taylor-Rostow mission, the Vietnam problem passed in effect from the Department of State to the Department of Defense, and, in spite of Kennedy's early insight into the political character of the problem in Vietnam, the projected American solution in 1961-1963 was increasingly framed in military terms. Why did Kennedy permit this to happen? One reason was that Vietnam was still in these years a low-level crisis. It was far less urgent than Cuba, or Berlin, or Latin America, or nuclear testing, or preserving the European alliance, or fighting for civil rights in the United States; far less urgent than the neighboring Asian crisis in Laos. Another reason was that the strategy of unconditional support of Diem combined with the military adviser system seemed to be working—or so at least the senior American officials in Saigon assured the President. Their dispatches conveyed the picture of a regime led by a doubtless difficult but unquestionably statesmanlike and, in any case, irreplaceable figure making steady progress in winning over the peasants, pacifying the countryside and restoring the stability of government. If there was no surge of social reform, at least the "strategic hamlet" program—the relocation of peasants into fortified villages, surrounded by barbed wire fences and ditches filled with bamboo spikes—was giving the countryside protection and a new sense of security and cutting off the Viet Cong from their primary sources of food, intelligence and recruits. Ngo Dinh Nhu made the strategic hamlet program his personal project and published glowing reports of spectacular success. One might have wondered whether Nhu was just the man to mobilize the idealism of the villages; but Ambassador Nolting and General Harkins listened uncritically to his claims and passed them back to Washington as facts, where they were read with elation.

Washington officials on hasty visits confirmed the picture. "Every quantitative measurement we have," Secretary of Defense McNamara said on his first trip to Vietnam in 1962, "shows we're winning this war." General Taylor, when he returned for a fresh look a year after his first mission, detected "a great national movement" rising to destroy the Viet Cong. It was hard to doubt a widespread and substantial improvement in the military situation. The President, who had other matters on his mind, accepted the cheerful reports from men in whom he had great confidence. His 1963 State of the Union message summed up the mood at the turn of the year: "The spearpoint of aggression has been blunted in South Vietnam."

The optimism continued well into 1963. In March the Secretary of State said that the war was "turning an important corner. . . . Government forces clearly have the initiative in most areas of the country." A month later he discerned a "steady movement toward a constitutional system resting upon popular consent," declared that "the 'strategic hamlet' program is producing excellent results," added that "morale in the countryside has begun to rise," assured his listeners that "to the Vietnamese peasant" the Viet Cong "look less and less like winners" and concluded, "The Vietnamese are on their way to success" (meaning presumably the South Vietnamese). In May the Defense Department announced, "The corner has definitely been turned toward victory in Vietnam." General Harkins predicted that the war would be won "within a year." "South Vietnam," said

Ambassador Nolting in June, "is on its way to victory over communist guerrillas." "I can safely say," General Harkins unsafely said in October, "the end of the war is in sight."

There was another view of the situation—a view transmitted not in top secret cables but in dispatches to American newspapers and magazines.[5] The American reporters in Vietnam saw Diem not as a selfless national leader but as an oriental despot, hypnotized by his own endless monologues and contemptuous of democracy and the west. They detested the Nhus. They considered the strategic hamlet program a fake and a failure; and their visits to dismal stockades where peasants had been herded, sometimes at bayonet point, to engage in forced labor confirmed their worst misgivings. They stopped believing Diem's communiqués; and, when Harkins and Nolting kept insisting they were true, they stopped believing Harkins and Nolting. Their picture of South Vietnam differed from the official reports by about 180 degrees.

In response, the officials assailed the journalists. Admiral Felt, the commander of the Pacific fleet, reproached the man from the Associated Press: "Why don't you get on the team?" In reports to Washington the officials even gave the astonishing impression that there would be no trouble in Vietnam if only the newspaper fellows would follow the line. "The U.S. Embassy," wrote David Halberstam of the *New York Times,* who later won a Pulitzer Prize for his work in Vietnam, "turned into the adjunct of a dictatorship. In trying to protect Diem from criticism, the Ambassador became Diem's agent." One experience after another made the newspapermen more certain that the Embassy was lying to them. They did not recognize the deeper pathos, which was that the officials really believed their

[5] This should console those who feel they are deprived of something if denied access to top secret dispatches.

own reports. They were deceiving not only the American government and people but themselves.

Then in May 1963 Diem forbade the Buddhists to display their flags on Buddha's 2587th birthday, Diem's troops fired into a crowd of Buddhists in Hue, and the situation suddenly fell apart. The Buddhist trouble was as much social as religious in its impulse. It was at bottom an uprising, wholly unforeseen by American diplomats, of the new generation of nationalists, drawn largely from the middle and lower classes, speaking Vietnamese rather than French, professing Buddhism rather than Catholicism, xenophobic and hysterical, in revolt against traditional Vietnamese society. Diem and the Nhus retaliated with equal hysteria. The result was to expose the optimism that had been flowing so long and so imperturbably out of American officials in Saigon and to strengthen those few officials in Washington —notably Averell Harriman, Under Secretary of State, and Roger Hilsman, Assistant Secretary for Far Eastern Affairs, who for some time had been questioning the orthodox picture. The appointment of Henry Cabot Lodge as Ambassador to Saigon reinforced the skeptics.

The Buddhist troubles finally made Vietnam a matter of top priority, even in the months of Bull Connor and his police dogs in Birmingham, of the American University speech and the test ban treaty, of the fight for tax reduction and the civil rights bill. "In my opinion," Kennedy said, "for us to withdraw from that effort would mean a collapse not only of South Vietnam but Southeast Asia. So we are going to stay there." But he could not forget the French experience of a decade earlier; if the war were ever converted into a white man's war, the Americans would lose as the French had lost. "In the final analysis," he said on September 3, "it is their war. They are the ones who have to win it or lose it. We can help them, we can give them equipment, we can send our men out there as advisers, but they have to win it, the people of Vietnam."

Finally the South Vietnamese army brought off its

coup, killed Diem and Nhu, and the war entered a new phase. Three weeks later Kennedy too was dead, and a new President inherited the trouble. Vietnam was still not a top problem. In his first State of the Union message, President Johnson hardly mentioned Vietnam.[6] In his 1965 message, Vietnam received hardly more than 100 words. Even his 1966 message took thirty-five minutes before there was any extended discussion of Vietnam. It is important to remember how long it was before Vietnam emerged as the all-consuming and all-dominating issue it is today.

It did, however, play a role in the 1964 election, largely because of Senator Goldwater's advocacy of an aggressive northern strategy. President Johnson replied:

> Some others are eager to enlarge the conflict. They call upon us to supply American boys to do the job that Asian boys should do. They ask us to take reckless actions which might risk the lives of millions and engulf much of Asia.
>
> (August 12)

> I have had advice to load our planes with bombs and to drop them on certain areas that I think would enlarge the war and result in committing a good many American boys to fighting a war that I think ought to be fought by the boys of Asia to help protect their own land. And for that reason I haven't chosen to enlarge the war.
>
> (August 29)

> There are those that say you ought to go north and drop bombs, to try to wipe out the supply lines, and

[6] The two references in the message of January 8, 1964, were speech-writer's reflexes: "Today Americans of all races stand side by side in Berlin and in Vietnam" (in a passage on civil rights) and "In 1964 we will be better prepared than ever before to defend the cause of freedom—whether it is threatened by outright aggression or by the infiltration practiced by those in Hanoi and Havana" (in a passage on national security policy).

they think that would escalate the war. We don't want our American boys to do the fighting for Asian boys. We don't want to get involved in a nation with 700 million people and get tied down in a land war in Asia.

(September 25)

We are not going north and we are not going south; we are going to continue to try to get them to save their own freedom with their own men, with our leadership and our officer direction, and such equipment as we can furnish them.

(September 28)

We are not going to send American boys nine or ten thousand miles away from home to do what Asian boys ought to be doing for themselves.

(October 21)

III

WHERE WE ARE NOW

*C*AMPAIGN SPEECHES are not sacred covenants with the people; they are expressions of intent and hope, and there is no reason to question the honesty of President Johnson's 1964 statements.[1] What the President apparently did not allow for was a continued decay in the military situation. Things became so desperate in the early months of 1965—or so we were later told—that only the February decision to start bombing the north, followed by the commitment of American combat forces the next month, averted total collapse. If the situation was really all that grave, the administration did not confide this fact at the time to the American people; in retrospect, one simply does not know whether this story is actuality or myth. If actuality, it might surely have called Washington's attention to the political weaknesses of the Saigon regime; for the South Vietnamese

[1] However, Charles Roberts, the White House correspondent of *Newsweek,* wrote in his book, *LBJ's Inner Circle,* "The President . . . told me in May 1965 that he had made the decision to bomb [North Vietnam] . . . four months before Pleiku." This would place the decision in October 1964. But the President's wording may have been loose or his memory faulty; for I know of no other indication that the decision was in fact taken that early.

Army at this point still outnumbered the Viet Cong by at least six to one, and its capitulation would have been more an expression of political demoralization than of military inferiority.

In any case, the President now felt he had no alternative but to begin to supply American boys to do the job that he had thought a few months before Asian boys should do. The number of American troops doubled, and doubled again; by August 1965 there were 125,000. The bombing steadily grew, except for a meaningless six-day pause in May. As we increased our activity, Hanoi reciprocated. According to our estimates, the enemy amounted to 90,000 in March 1964; 100,000 in January 1965; and, after the active American entry into the war, 135,000 by April and 170,000 by August. In December 1965 the United States instituted a second bombing pause. After thirty-seven days, the process of escalation resumed. By the end of 1966 the number of American troops was rising toward 400,000. As for the bombing of the north, there were 1935 missions in February 1966, 5183 in April, 7357 in June, 9765 in July, 12,673 in September.

And so the policy of 'one more step' lured the United States deeper and deeper into the morass. In retrospect, Vietnam is a triumph of the politics of inadvertence. We have achieved our present entanglement, not after due and deliberate consideration, but through a series of small decisions. It is not only idle but unfair to seek out guilty men. President Eisenhower, after rejecting American military intervention in 1954, set in motion the policy of support for Saigon which resulted, two Presidents later, in American military intervention in 1965. Each step in the deepening of the American commitment was reasonably regarded at the time as the last that would be necessary. Yet, in retrospect, each step led only to the next, until we find ourselves entrapped today in that nightmare of American strategists, a land war in Asia—a war which no President, including President Johnson, desired or intended. The Vietnam story is a tragedy without villains. No thoughtful American can withhold sympathy as President Johnson ponders the gloomy choices which lie ahead.

Yet each President, in the words of Andrew Jackson, remains "accountable at the bar of public opinion for every act of his administration." President Johnson has made his ultimate objective very clear: he does not seek, he has said, total military victory or the unconditional surrender of North Vietnam,[2] but a negotiated settlement. He has also made very clear his judgment that the way to achieve a political solution is by intensifying military pressure until a battered and reeling Hanoi agrees to negotiate—or, at least, pulls out its forces and allows the war to fade away. By continually increasing what the Pentagon calls the "quotient of pain," we can, according to the administration theory, force Hanoi at each stage of widening the war to reconsider whether the war is worth the price.

This has been the persistent administration course since February 1965. New experiments in escalation are first denied, then disowned, then discounted and finally undertaken. Thus in the early winter of 1965 the Secretary of Defense told Congress that bombing the petroleum facilities near Haiphong was of "no fundamental consequence"; in the spring the Secretary of the Air Force explained why we were not going to bomb Hanoi and Haiphong; on June 26, the Under Secretary of State denied that any decision had been taken to bomb the oil storage depots; on June 29, the bombing began. For a moment Washington put out stories suggesting that this was going to be some sort of turning point in the war. High officials cited unidentified intelligence dispatches reporting the decline of morale in North Vietnam. But in the months since it has become evident that, once again, the newest step in escalation made no more difference than the previous steps.

[2] One must discount flourishes like the presidential exhortation to the combat commanders in the officers' club at Camranh Bay: "Come home with that coonskin on the wall."

So, once again, the demand arises for 'just one *more* step.' As past medicine fails, all we can apparently think to do is to double the dose. Plenty of room remains for widening the war: the harbors of North Vietnam, the irrigation dikes, the steel plants, the factories, the power grid, the crops, the civilian population, the Chinese border. The fact that we excluded such steps yesterday is, alas, no guarantee that we will not pursue them tomorrow. And if bombing will not bring Ho Chi Minh to his knees or stop his support of the Viet Cong in South Vietnam, there is always the resort of invasion. General Ky has already told us that we must invade North Vietnam to win the war. In an August press conference, the Secretary of State twice refused to rule out this possibility. And beyond invasion lies the field of nuclear weapons—weapons which General Eisenhower, who declined the conventional bombing of Dien Bien Phu in 1954, would not exclude in 1966.

The theory, of course, is that widening the war will shorten it. This theory appears to be based on three convictions: first, that the war will be decided in North Vietnam; second, that the risk of Chinese or Soviet entry is negligible; and third, that military 'victory' in some sense is possible—not perhaps total victory over North Vietnam but suppression of resistance in South Vietnam. Perhaps these premises are correct, and in another year or two we may all be saluting the wisdom and statesmanship of the American government. In so enigmatic a situation, no one can be confident about his doubt and disagreement. Nonetheless, to many Americans these propositions constitute a terribly shaky basis for action which has already carried the United States into a ground war in Asia and which may well carry the world to the brink of the third world war.

The illusion that the war in South Vietnam can be decided in North Vietnam is evidently a result of listening too long to our own propaganda. "The war," the Secretary of State has solemnly assured us, "is clearly an 'armed attack,' cynically and systematically mounted by the Hanoi regime against the people of South Vietnam." Our government has insisted so often that the war in South Vietnam is, in President Johnson's phrase, "a vicious and illegal aggression across this little nation's frontier," that it has come to believe itself that the war was started in Hanoi and can only be stopped there.

Yet the best evidence remains that the war began as an insurrection within South Vietnam which, as it has gathered momentum, has attracted increasing support and direction from the north. In August 1966, four correspondents who had been covering the Vietnam war —Malcolm Browne of the Associated Press (whose book on Vietnam, *The New Face of War,* had won the Pulitzer Prize), Jack Foisie of the *Los Angeles Times* (who is the Secretary of State's brother-in-law), Charles Mohr of the *New York Times* and Dean Brelis of the National Broadcasting Company—discussed this point:

> BROWNE: Of course, it is a civil war, by the Webster definition of the thing.
> NIVEN (moderator): So you all agree?
> FOISIE: I think it is.
> BRELIS: Yes, I agree.
> MOHR: Yes, a special kind of civil war.

Even today the North Vietnamese regulars in South Vietnam amount to only a small fraction of the total enemy force (and to an even smaller fraction of the American army in South Vietnam). We could follow the genial prescription of General LeMay and bomb North Vietnam back to the Stone Age—and the war would still go on in South Vietnam. To reduce this war to the simplification of a wicked regime molesting its neighbors, and to suppose that it can be ended by punishing the wicked regime, is surely to misconceive not only the political but even the military character of the problem.

As for the assurances that China will not enter, these will be less than totally satisfying to those whose memory stretches back to the Korean War. General Mac-

Arthur, another one of those military experts on oriental psychology, when asked by President Truman on Wake Island in October 1950 what the chances were of Chinese intervention, replied, "Very little. . . . Now that we have bases for our Air Force in Korea, if the Chinese tried to get down to Pyongyang, there would be the greatest slaughter." Such reasoning lay behind the decision (the Assistant Secretary of State for Far Eastern Affairs at that time is Secretary of State today) to send American troops across the 38th parallel despite warnings from Peking that this would provoke a Chinese response. In a few weeks, China was actively in the war, and, while there was the greatest slaughter, it was not notably of the Chinese.

There seems little question that the Chinese have no great passion to enter the war in Vietnam. They do not want to put their nuclear plants in hazard; and, in any case, their foreign policy has typically been a compound of polemical ferocity and practical prudence. But it is essential, if we seek to assess Chinese policy realistically, to make the big effort and try to grasp the problem as it appears to them. Liddell Hart once wrote, in a passage cherished by John F. Kennedy, "Never corner an opponent, and always assist him to save his face. Put yourself in his shoes—so as to see things through his eyes. Avoid self-righteousness like the devil—nothing is so self-blinding." Such precepts are infuriating to the moralists of diplomacy, who believe that foreign policy is essentially about questions of right and wrong. They are, however, indispensable to statesmen.

What, therefore, is the view from Peking? It is obviously of a gigantic American effort at the encirclement and strangulation of China. That is not, of course, our view of what we are doing; nor is it in fact what we are doing. But it really should not astonish us that a crew of dogmatic Marxist-Leninists should so interpret the extraordinary deployment of American armies, navies and military bases thousands of miles from the United States and mobilized—on the word of American leaders—

against no one but themselves. Imagine our own feelings if the Chinese had 400,000 troops in southern Mexico, engaged in putting down what we had hoped to be a pro-American rebellion; if massive Chinese military bases were being built there; if Chinese planes were bombing northern Mexico every day; if a great Chinese fleet controlled the waters along our Pacific coast; and if Peking was denouncing the United States as the world's greatest threat to peace. The question, which so engages on our own sense of righteousness, of who the 'aggressor' is, depends a good deal on who looks through what glass and how darkly. The leaders in Peking are fully as devoted students of Munich as the American Secretary of State.[3] They are sure that we are out to bury them; they believe too that appeasement invites further aggression; and, however deep their reluctance, at some point concern for national survival will make them fight. "To save our neighbors," as Peking announced on November 4, 1950, "is to save ourselves."

When will that point be reached this time? Probably when the Chinese are confronted by a direct threat to their frontier, either through bombing or through an American decision to cross the 17th parallel and invade North Vietnam. If a Communist regime barely established in Peking could take a decision to intervene against the only atomic power in the world in 1950, why does anyone suppose that a much stronger regime would flinch from that decision in 1966? Indeed, given the present discord in Peking, war may seem the best way to renew revolutionary discipline, stop the brawling and unite the nation.

It is true that the Chinese entry into the Korean War had the support of the Soviet Union; but it would be risky today to rely on the Russo-Chinese split to save us from everything, including Soviet aid to China in case

[3] General Lo Jui-ching, in his introduction to Marshal Lin Piao's 1965 manifesto, invokes the Munich analogy three times; see the recent book by Brigadier General Samuel B. Griffith II, *Peking and People's Wars* (New York, 1966).

of war with the United States or even direct Soviet entry into the war in Vietnam. For the Soviet Union is already extensively involved in Vietnam—more so in a sense than the Chinese—and it is foolish to suppose that, given Moscow's competition with Peking for the leadership of the Communist world, Russia could afford to stand by and allow Communist North Vietnam or Communist China to be destroyed by the American imperialists.

And if China does enter? Once again, the bombing illusion, the bane of American popular thought on military matters; I suppose we will be exhorted to blast China back to the Stone Age too. But, as General Ridgway pointed out a decade ago, the Chinese "are not yet sufficiently 'advanced' to be truly vulnerable to the nuclear bomb. . . . Their civilization is not based on a complex nerve fabric, a web of interrelated and interdependent functions and services, as is ours. Theirs is a simpler and more primitive society that would be extremely difficult to destroy, just as the turtle and the crocodile are harder to kill than the higher animals." General Ridgway also questioned the morality of nuclear bombing—all the more relevant too, if we seem to reserve our most ghastly weapon for yellow people. China can be defeated only on the ground—and the Chinese will have a good many more foot soldiers than the United States to throw into any conflict.[4]

This consideration relates to the third premise: that military 'victory' is in some sense possible. The Joint Chiefs of Staff, of course, by definition argue for military solutions. They are the most fervent apostles of 'one more step.' That is their business, and no one should be surprised that generals behave like generals. The

[4] One should perhaps record General LeMay's solution to this problem as an indication of the infinite capacity of the military mind for self-deception. "We need never invade with our own land forces. Air, naval and logistic support to Chiang Kai-shek on Formosa and General Chung Hee Park in South Korea should provide more than enough force to bring an unstable Red China to her knees."

fault lies not with those who give this advice but those who take it. There is nothing infallible about the Chiefs, as anyone who recalls their counsel at the time of the Bay of Pigs and again during the Cuban missile crisis well knows. Their recommendations, even on strictly military questions, deserve the most hard and skeptical analysis.

What, for example, is the exact purpose of bombing the north? It is difficult to find out. According to General Taylor, "The objective of our air campaign is to change the will of the enemy leadership." Secretary McNamara, on the other hand, has said, "We never believed that bombing would destroy North Vietnam's will." He told the Chamber of Commerce in May 1966 that, since North Vietnam was largely agricultural, with only 15 per cent of its gross national product coming from industry, it was "impossible" to bring the nation's economy "to a halt" through bombing. Whatever the theory, the results would appear to support Secretary McNamara. "There is no indication," General Westmoreland said in August 1966, "that the resolve of the leadership in Hanoi has been reduced." In other words, bombing has had precisely the effect that the analyses of the United States Strategic Bombing Survey after the Second World War would have forecast. Under Secretary of State George Ball was a director of that Survey; this may well be why he has been reported to be so unenthusiastic about the air assault on the north.

And, far from stopping infiltration across the 17th parallel, bombing, if our own reports are to be believed, has stimulated it. The first result was to bring North Vietnamese forces south of the border. "In 1965," according to General Westmoreland, "[the enemy] began to move regular North Vietnamese Army units into [South] Vietnam." "It is perfectly clear," Secretary McNamara has said, "that the North Vietnamese have continued to increase their support of the Viet Cong despite the increase in our effort. . . . What has happened is that the North Vietnamese have continually increased the amount of resources, men and material that they have been willing to devote to their objective." In May 1966, after fourteen months of bombing, Secretary McNamara said that the infiltration rate was "perhaps three times the level of last year"; in June he said that Communist supply deliveries had risen by 150 per cent and troop infiltration by 120 per cent over the previous year; and each month we are told, the rates continue to rise. Talk about bombing the "Ho Chi Minh Trail," for example, is misleading; it is not a broad highway accessible to aircraft but a maze of threads through the jungle; and, even if our planes were to knock out the North Vietnamese trucks, bearers could if necessary carry the amount needed to maintain Viet Cong operations at their present level. (No one knows what this amount is; Secretary McNamara has estimated it as twelve to thirty tons a day in 1965.) Bombing undoubtedly makes infiltration more difficult, but its effects are transient, and it will not bring infiltration to an end.

Moreover, far from discouraging external assistance to North Vietnam, our bombing has made Russian and Chinese aid to Hanoi a matter of Communist competition and honor. Russian exports to North Vietnam, for example, increased sharply (from 42.9 million rubles in 1964 to 67.4 million rubles in 1965) after we began to bomb the north. Richard N. Goodwin, a former special assistant to Presidents Kennedy and Johnson has said, "The increase in Soviet and Chinese aid, since the bombing, is far greater, in economic terms, than the loss through bombing. Except in human life, the North Vietnamese are showing a profit."

U.S. News & World Report remarked in its issue of August 22, 1966: "It's clear now to military men: bombing will not win in Vietnam." This is a dispiriting item. Why had our military leaders not long ago freed themselves from the illusion of the omnipotence of air power, so cherished by civilians who think wars can be won on the cheap? The Korean War, as General Ridgway has reminded us, "taught that it is impossible to interdict the supply route of an Asian army by airpower alone. We had complete air mastery over North Korea, and we clobbered Chinese supply columns unmercifully. . . . But we did not halt their offensive nor materially diminish its strength." If air power was not decisive in Korea, where the warfare was conventional and the terrain relatively open and compact, how could anyone suppose that it would be decisive against guerrillas threading their way through the hills and jungles of Vietnam?

No doubt killing a lot of North Vietnamese may give some Americans inner psychic satisfaction. But the hard question is whether it will help 'win' the war. The evidence thus far is that bombing the north, instead of demoralizing North Vietnam, stopping the infiltration and the foreign aid, driving a wedge between Hanoi and Peking and hurrying Hanoi to the conference table, has stimulated infiltration and assistance, hardened the will of the regime, convinced it that its life is at stake, brought it closer to China and solidified the people of North Vietnam in its support. Meanwhile it has had little effect on the real war—which, after all, is taking place not in the north but in the south.

Victory through bombing—the dream of an antiseptic war and a painless triumph—is a cruel form of self-deception. Those who think total military victory the proper goal must have the moral and intellectual honesty (as, for example, Hanson Baldwin has) to face the probability that it can come only in South Vietnam and only through ground warfare. The bombing illusion applies, of course, to South as well as to North Vietnam. Tactical bombing—bombing in direct support of ground operations—has its place; but the notion that strategic bombing can stop guerrillas runs contrary to experience. And we have it, on the authority of the Secretary of State, that despite the entry of North Vietnamese regulars the war in South Vietnam (as of early 1966) "continues to be basically a guerrilla operation."

Sir Robert Thompson, who planned the successful British effort against the Malayan guerrillas and later served as head of the British advisory mission in Saigon, has emphasized that in guerrilla warfare the defending force must operate "in the same element" as their adversaries. Counter-insurgency, he writes, "is like trying to deal with a tomcat in an alley. It is no good inserting a large, fierce dog. The dog may not find the tomcat; if he does, the tomcat will escape up a tree; and the dog will then chase the female cats. The answer is to put in a fiercer tomcat."

Alas, we have no fiercer tomcat. Kennedy's counter-insurgency effort in Vietnam has languished. Today we fight one war, with our B-52's and our naval guns and our napalm, and the Viet Cong are fighting another, with their machine guns and ambushes and forays in the dark. Our men in Saigon claim that Viet Cong morale is sinking under the pounding. A brilliant and informed columnist writes (in October 1966), "Within six, eight, ten or twelve months—before the end of 1967 at any rate—the chances are good that the Vietnamese war will look successful. We are much closer to the end of . . . the 'military war' than most people . . . dare to hope." We all pray that Mr. Alsop will be right. But that corner in Vietnam has been turned too often before.

"If we can get the Viet Cong to stand up and fight, we will blast him," General Westmoreland has plaintively said; and when they occasionally rise to the surface and try to fight our kind of war, we do blast them. But the fact that they then slide back into the shadows does not mean that we are on the verge of some final military triumph. It means simply that we are driving them underground—where they renew themselves and where our large, fierce dog cannot follow. "When we have beaten the Army of North Vietnam and the main-force battalions of the Viet Cong," Ambassador Lodge said in November 1966, "we have simply won the opportunity to get at the heart of the matter, which is more than 150,000 terrorist guerrillas highly organized throughout the country and looking exactly like civilians." Or, as General Moshe Dayan, who led the Israeli Army in the 1956 campaign against Egypt, put it after a visit to Vietnam: "The Viet Cong army can, if it refrains from pitting regular units against regular units in frontal engagements and organizes guerrilla warfare, prevent the Americans and the Saigon government from pacifying the country. The Viet Cong cannot drive out the Americans, but they can, by adopting appropriate methods of warfare, avoid being driven out themselves."

As for the alleged collapse of guerrilla morale, there has thus far been no convincing evidence that the Viet Cong lack the political and emotional commitment to keep fighting underground for a very long time. Neil Sheehan of the *New York Times* wrote in his valedictory piece about Vietnam: "We are continually chagrined to discover that idealism and dedication are largely the prerogative of the enemy. . . . I can only conclude that Vietnamese will die more willingly for a regime which, though Communist, is at least genuinely Vietnamese and offers them some hope of improving their lives, than for one which is committed to the galling status quo and is the creation of Washington." Ellen Hammer in her book of 1954, *The Struggle for Indochina,* reminds us of the ancient boast of the Vietnamese nationalists: "We have fought for a thousand years. And we will fight another thousand if need be."

Nor can we easily match the continuing infiltration by enlarging our own forces—from 300,000, for example, to 500,000 or 750,000. The ratio of superiority preferred by the Pentagon in guerrilla war is 10 to 1, which means that every time we send in 100,000 more men the enemy has only to send in 10,000 or so, and we are all even again. Reinforcement has not created a margin of American superiority; all it has done is to lift the stalemate to a higher and more explosive level. Indeed, there is reason to suppose that, in its own manner, the enemy can match our every step of escalation up to the point of nuclear war. And, should we attempt to root out the guerrillas in every village and cave, it would require almost a million American soldiers and a war of many years. Such an effort would hopelessly Americanize the war, transforming it from a conflict between nationalist and Communist Vietnamese into the white man's war which President Kennedy feared. It would hopelessly militarize the problem, diverting all thought and energy from the search for a political solution. The sheer weight of the American military presence would overwhelm the social structure of Vietnam, corrupt its way of life,[5] smother its national identity and produce in reaction an increasingly dangerous mood of anti-Americanism.

Meanwhile, as the number of our planes, our cannon and our ships increase, they will inevitably be thrown into battle. Already our bombers roam over the hapless country, dumping more tonnage of explosives each month than we were dropping per month on all Europe and Africa during the Second World War—more in a year than we dropped in the entire Pacific during the Second World War. Just the other day our bombs killed or injured more than one hundred civilians in a hamlet in the Mekong Delta—all on the suspicion that two Viet Cong platoons, numbering perhaps sixty men, were there. Even if the Viet Cong had still been around, which they weren't, would the military gain have outweighed the human and political loss? General Dayan describes a small action where, "along the 200-yard-wide strip between jungle and fence the American sup-

[5] "Corruption Is Taking Up to 40% of U.S. Assistance in Vietnam"—headline in *New York Times*, November 13, 1966. The piece begins "among the traditional by products of war are theft, bribery, black marketing, currency manipulation and waste. In the Vietnamese conflict these corrosive influences . . . have developed on a scale far vaster than should be expected for the size of the war." American officials, in challenging the 40 per cent estimate, concede "corruption and thievery to the extent that $35 million to $40 million worth of American commodities would be lost in Vietnam in the current fiscal year."

port units laid down no less than 21,000 shells—more than the total volume of artillery fire expended by the Israeli Army during the Suez Campaign and the War of Independence together!"[6] General Johnson, the Army Chief of Staff, observed unhappily to Dayan: "We have not enough information. We act with ruthlessness, like a steamroller, bombing extensive areas and not selected targets based on detailed intelligence." Charles Mohr has described in the *Times* the human consequences of this military promiscuity: "Almost every provincial hospital in Vietnam is crowded with civilian victims of the war. Some American doctors and other officials in the field say the majority are the victims of American air power and South Vietnamese artillery."

Our strategy in Vietnam today is rather like trying to weed a garden with a bulldozer. We occasionally dig up some weeds, but we dig up most of the turf, too. If we continue the pursuit of total military victory, we will leave the tragic country gutted and devastated by bombs, burned by napalm, turned into a wasteland by chemical defoliation, a land of ruin and wreck. This is the melancholy course to which the escalation policy commits us. The effect will be to pulverize the political and institutional fabric which alone can give a South Vietnamese state that hope of independent survival which is our presumed war aim. Our method, in other words, defeats

---

[6] Nor does all our devastation land on verified military targets. According to Neil Sheehan, "Hamlets are also habitually bombed and shelled at the request of a South Vietnamese province or district chief who has been told by some paid informer that Communist troops are present there. Information from informers is notoriously unreliable, the peasants are often not responsible for the presence of the Communists and, since ground units do not exploit the bombings and shellings, these attacks seem to have negligible military value. American officials excuse the practice by claiming that the Vietnamese, as the legal authorities, have the right to destroy their own hamlets. . . . I have occasionally thought that the practice results largely from the cynicism of South Vietnamese officialdom and a superfluity of aircraft and artillery."

our goal. Indeed, the most likely beneficiary of the smashed social structure of South Vietnam will be communism. In our wisdom we are creating the only conditions in which China could easily take over Vietnam. "In another day," Jean Lacouture has written, "Mongol emperors sacked and massacred Asian peoples before subjugating them. In Vietnam the first part of the job would then have been done by the Americans."

"My feeling," General Wallace Greene, commandant of the Marine Corps, has wisely said, "is that you could kill every Viet Cong and North Vietnamese in South Vietnam and still lose the war. Unless we can make a success of the civic-action program, we are not going to obtain the objectives we have set." Much devotion and intelligence are at present going into the programs of reconstruction and pacification. But two factors hold up the social revolution in South Vietnam: the capacity of the enemy to slice through so much of the country with relative immunity; and, equally important, the resistance of the large landholders and leading elements in the Saigon government to any serious programs of social reform. In any case, as claimants on our resources, these programs are hopelessly outclassed by the programs of destruction. Surely the United States, with all its ingenuity could have figured out a better way to combat guerrilla warfare than the physical obliteration of the nation in which that warfare is taking place. If this is our best idea of 'protecting' a country against 'wars of national liberation,' what other country, seeing the devastation we have wrought in Vietnam, will wish American protection? What will happen to the credibility of our commitments then?[7]

And there is a deeper question, a question which al-

---

[7] "We are here because we made a promise. We have made other promises in other parts of the world. If Moscow or Peking ever discover that the promises of the United States do not mean what they say, then this world goes up in smoke"— the Secretary of State during his visit to Vietnam in October 1966.

ready haunts the American conscience. Are we really carrying out this policy, as we constantly proclaim, to save the people we are methodically destroying, or are we doing it for less exalted purposes of our own? Are we treating the Vietnamese as ends in themselves, or as means to our own objectives? The war began as a struggle for the soul of Vietnam: will it end as a struggle for the soul of America?

IV

THE PRICE WE ARE PAYING

*O*UR CONCENTRATION on Vietnam is exacting a frightful cost. In domestic policy, with Vietnam gulping down more than a billion and a half dollars a month, everything is grinding to a stop. Lyndon Johnson was on his way to a place in history as a great President for his vision of a Great Society; but the Great Society is now, except for token gestures, dead. The fight for equal opportunity for the Negro, the war against poverty, the struggle to save the cities, the improvement of our schools—all must be starved for the sake of Vietnam. And war brings ugly side-effects: inflation; frustration; indignation; protest; panic; angry divisions within the national community; premonitions of McCarthyism.

American public opinion, the Louis Harris poll tells us, "is rising toward increased militancy about the Vietnam war and a get-it-over-with mood." No doubt this is so: the fear of a hopeless stalemate in Southeast Asia has produced a hunger for drastic solutions. It is not so much hawks vs. doves any longer as it is people becoming simultaneously hawks *and* doves and saying, like Senator Russell, that "we should go in and win—or else get out." Among the early casualties of this get-it-over-with frenzy are likely to be our national equability, good temper, moderation and reason. And, as the frenzy gathers speed, it may well bring in its wake a new testing of the national faith in liberty.

The last such testing took place fifteen years ago. The more venerable among us may still recall the havoc—so absurd in retrospect—which a single senator then wrought in the workings of our government and the atmosphere of our society. Now, though he was unquestionably talented as a demagogue, it was not the quality of his demagoguery alone which gave Senator McCarthy his influence. It was the fact that his demagoguery incited and interpreted acute hostilities and frustrations among the American people, hostilities and frustrations generated, in the main, by our participation in the war in Korea.

All wars generate frustrations, but the Korean War was peculiarly frustrating. It was a limited war, and, though the reasons for its limitations were cogent, they were imperfectly understood by many Americans. This meant that there was spreading incomprehension and resentment over the fact that, as casualty lists lengthened, our government, renouncing nuclear weapons and respecting privileged sanctuaries, stubbornly declined to unleash the full force of our military power against the enemy. Moreover, if Communists were killing Americans in Korea, why should Americans be expected to tolerate for a moment any one at home who could be said to sound or look like a Communist? And some Americans who perhaps felt they ought to be in Korea themselves found it easy to expiate their guilt and affirm their virility by joining Senator McCarthy's anti-Communist crusade. As a result, so long as the Korean War continued, McCarthy was able to influence a considerable number of his fellow citizens. He rode high in these years, leaving behind a trail of mistrust, fear and ruin. It was not till 1953, when the Korean armistice concluded the frustrations on which the Senator thrived, that the nation began to slip the bondage to hysteria and awaken from the nightmare.

The Vietnam war is just as frustrating as the Korean War and a good deal harder for most people to understand. The Korean War, after all, was a clear-cut case of invasion across frontiers; it entirely lacked the dimension of internal revolt which gives the struggle in Vietnam its peculiar difficulties. Moreover, the United States fought in Korea as the representative of the United Nations with the unqualified blessing of most of the world, while today we fight in Vietnam substantially alone. Then we had a relatively stable local government as our partner in Seoul—as against the parade of regimes in recent years in Saigon, many engaged in warfare against their own people. And then communism still seemed a united and mortal world threat, demanding the most urgent response—while today, as it degenerates into a scramble of warring tongs, it is losing its power and its momentum.

For all these reasons, the war in Vietnam may, in time, generate a higher intensity of frustration than the Korean War. And, if history repeats itself—and history sometimes does[1]—the war in Vietnam might well produce something roughly comparable to the McCarthy phenomenon of 1950-1954. As draft calls enlarge, as more soldiers disembark in Saigon, as casualties mount, as the war increasingly dominates and obsesses our national life, we can look for the appearance of associated symptoms: the oversimplification and emotionalization of issues, the exchange of invective—one side becoming 'warmongers,' the other 'appeasers'—the questioning of motives and of loyalties and the degradation of debate.

As this process continues, the emotional advantage will be increasingly on the side of the flag-wavers. Some of these will be tempted to pay off old scores as they wrap themselves in Old Glory. Conservative congressmen are already using the war in Vietnam as the excuse

[1] With qualifications noted below; see Chapter VII.

to oppose Great Society legislation which they would have opposed anyway; soon it may become a club with which they can assault old time liberal antagonists. Mark Twain described the process years ago:

> The loud little handful—as usual—will shout for the war. . . . A few fair men on the other side will argue and reason against the war with speech and pen, and at first will have a hearing and be applauded, but it will not last long; those others will outshout them, and presently the anti-war audiences will thin out and lose popularity. Before long you will see this curious thing: the speakers stoned from the platform, the free speech strangled by hordes of furious men who in their hearts are still at one with the stoned speakers—as earlier— but do not dare to say so. And now the whole nation —pulpit and all—will take up the war-cry and shout itself hoarse, and mob any honest man who ventures to open his mouth, and presently such mouths will cease to open.

Patriotism may become again, as Edmund Burke once wrote, "a bloody idol, which required the sacrifice of children and parents, or dearest connexions in private life, and of all the virtues that arise from those relations."

Thus the Georgia legislature has already refused a seat to a man, twice duly elected, because it disapproves of his views on Vietnam. Thus an American Communist who had won our country's second highest decoration, the Distinguished Service Cross for extraordinary heroism in the Second World War, has been forbidden burial in Arlington Cemetery. Thus a lieutenant in the Army was sentenced to two years' imprisonment at hard labor (later reduced) and discharged from the service for taking part, while off duty and in civilian clothes, in a demonstration against the Vietnam war. Thus a ninth-grade teacher who stood silently during a flag salute at a school assembly because he did not agree with the Vietnam policy was expelled from the Las Vegas, Nevada, unit of the American Federation of Teachers, harried by anonymous phone calls and threatened with dismissal unless he promised to salute the flag in the future—which, after thirty-eight days, he did. Thus groups of protestors against the war have been beaten up in several cities; a federal judge in Philadelphia has demanded that all publicly supported colleges expel student protestors; various draft boards have terminated their deferments, presumably on the weird theory that military service is a punishment; and children, too young to be drafted, have been suspended from high schools in Cleveland and Pittsburgh for wearing black armbands in mourning for the dead in Vietnam. Thus Senator Eastland of Mississippi has introduced a bill conferring broad powers on the State Department to restrict travel by American citizens overseas—and the State Department has called for surveillance of an eminent Harvard professor on his trips abroad. A former Vice President of the United States has even detected the hand of the unsleeping Communist conspiracy in the fact that the DuBois Clubs—the Young Communist League of the 1960s, so called after W. E. DuBois, the Negro historian who joined the Communist Party before his death—should have been given a name sounding so much like that of the Boy's Club of America. This, according to the vigilant Mr. Nixon, was "an almost classic example of communist deception and duplicity."

These were still in 1966 relatively scattered incidents. The American Civil Liberties Union did not see "a clear pattern of repression" although such repression had "occurred too frequently to be classed as sporadic or isolated." But, as the sense of frustration grows, so too may these incidents. They can rapidly become the enemy of a responsible democracy. They may create a climate where people begin to refrain from saying what they believe lest they get into trouble. Before we know it, we may be developing an atmosphere which only requires a new McCarthy to become a new McCarthyism.

Vietnam thus exacts a heavy price at home. It exacts

a heavy price abroad as well. On any realistic assessment, Western Europe and Latin America are far more significant to American security than Southeast Asia. Yet the Vietnam obsession has stultified our policy and weakened our position in both these vital areas. In Europe, for example, television has brought the horrors of the war into European parlors; and many—perhaps most—Europeans agreed with General de Gaulle when he said, "We find it totally detestable that a small country should be bombed by a very big one." The result has been the rise of a new form of anti-Americanism, emotional rather than ideological, leading toward a serious estrangement between Europe and America. The sense of estrangement is reinforced by the spreading impression that the United States, in its preoccupation with Vietnam, has lost interest in its western allies; and it is given a sharp edge by the fear that we are heading down the road toward war with China. When we began to bomb the oil deposits, James Reston wrote, "There is now not a single major nation in the world that supports Mr. Johnson's latest adventure in Hanoi and Haiphong." As other nations seek to disengage themselves from what they regard as an impending and unnecessary conflict, the quasi-neutralism of leaders like De Gaulle gains new plausibility.

At the same time, the war has clouded the hope, once mildly promising, of progress toward a detente with the Soviet Union. It has delayed agreements to end underground nuclear testing and to stop the spread of nuclear weapons. It almost persuaded U Thant to resign as Secretary General of the United Nations; and it probably condemns the UN itself to a time of frustration and declining influence.

Above all, it has estranged us from the future. For the future of all countries, developed or underdeveloped, depends on their youth—their young lawyers, politicians, scientists, engineers, teachers, trade unionists. These were exactly the young men and women who at the start of the sixties were beginning to look on the

United States as the hope of the world; exactly those today who watch our course in Vietnam with perplexity, loathing and despair. It has become fashionable again in Washington to belittle this consequence of our Vietnam policy, to dismiss 'world opinion' in favor of the presumed realities of national power. But the American Presidents who have wielded the greatest power in the world—Wilson, Franklin Roosevelt and Kennedy—did so precisely because they never forgot that a basic element of national power is the capacity to move world opinion.

The administration has called the critics of its Vietnam policy 'neo-isolationists.' But surely the real neo-isolationists are those who have isolated the United States from its traditional allies and from the people of the world. "There is not a single independent state in Europe or in Asia," writes Mr. Lippmann, "which follows our lead. . . . No European government could survive today if it joined us on the battlefield. . . . As for the Asian peoples we are supposed to be saving, no independent Asian state—not Japan, India, Pakistan, Burma, Malaysia, Indonesia—is giving us even token support." It is the administration, and not its critics, which has raised the old nationalist standard, dropped fifteen years ago by Douglas MacArthur, of 'going it alone.' For unilateral action is the essence of isolationism, and this is increasingly the logic of our Vietnam policy.

V

THE ROOTS OF OUR TROUBLE

*H*OW HAVE WE MANAGED to imprison ourselves in this series of dilemmas? One reason is a resurgence of old illusions—the illusion of American omnipotence and the illusion of American omniscience.

Our rejection of the views of our friends and allies—our conviction, as Paul H. Smith has put it, "that we alone are qualified to be judge, jury and executioner"—ignores Madison's solemn warning in the 63rd Federalist:

> An attention to the judgment of other nations is important to every government for two reasons: the one is that independently of the merits of any particular plan or measure, it is desirable, on various accounts, that it should appear to other nations as the offspring of a wise and honorable policy; the second is that in doubtful cases, particularly where the national councils may be warped by some strong passion or momentary interest, the presumed or known opinion of the impartial world may be the best guide that can be followed. What has not America lost by her want of character with foreign nations; and how many errors and follies would she not have avoided, if the justice and propriety of her measures had, in every instance, been previously

tried by the light in which they would probably appear to be the unbiased part of mankind.

Or, as President Kennedy said many years later: "We must face the fact that the United States is neither omnipotent nor omniscient—that we are only six per cent of the world's population—that we cannot impose our will on the other ninety-four per cent of mankind —that we cannot right every wrong or reverse each adversity—and that therefore there cannot be an American solution to every world problem."

We have not only lost a sense of the limitations on our power but also our understanding of the uses of power. Understanding of power implies above all precision in its application. We have moved away from the subtle strategy of 'flexible response' under which the level of American force was graduated to meet the level of enemy threat. The triumph of this discriminate employment of power was, of course, the Cuban missile crisis (where the Joint Chiefs, as usual, urged an air assault on the missile bases). But President Johnson, for all his formidable abilities, has shown no knack for discrimination in his use of power. His technique is to try and overwhelm his adversary—as in the Dominican Republic and Vietnam—by piling on all forms of power without regard to the nature of the threat. His greatest weakness is his susceptibility to overkill.

Given this weakness, it is easy to see why the application of force in Vietnam has been surrendered to the workings of what an acute observer of the Johnson foreign policy, Philip Geyelin, calls "the escalation machine." This machine is, in effect, the momentum in the decision-making system which keeps on enlarging the war "for reasons only marginally related to military need."

The very size of the American military presence thus generates unceasing pressures to see all problems in military terms and to subordinate everything else to military demands. These may be demands to try out new weapons; the *London Sunday Telegraph* recently ran an informative article comparing the Vietnam war to the Spanish Civil War as a military testing ground and laboratory. Or they may be cries for 'one more step,' springing in part from suppressed rage over the fact that, with military power sufficient to blow up the world, we still cannot subdue guerrilla bands in black pajamas, without air power or artillery. Whatever the reason, Sir Robert Thompson has noted of the American theory of the war: "There was a constant tendency in Vietnam to mount large-scale operations, which had little purpose or prospect of success, merely to indicate that something aggressive was being done."

The administration has admitted that such operations, like the bombing of the north, are designed in part to prop up the morale of the Saigon government. And the impression is growing now that they are also in part undertaken in order to affect public opinion in the United States and to reverse anti-administration tendencies in the polls. Americans have become curiously insensitive to the use of military operations for domestic political purposes. A quarter-century ago President Roosevelt postponed the North African invasion so that it would not take place before the mid-term elections of 1942; but today observers in Washington, without evidence of dismay, freely ascribe escalation to national politics.

The triumph of the escalation machine has been assisted by the faultiness of the information on which our decisions are based. Nothing is phonier than the spurious exactitude of our statistics about the Vietnam war. No doubt a computerized military establishment demands numbers; but the "body count" of dead Viet Cong, for example, includes heaven knows how many innocent bystanders and could hardly be more unreliable. So in the spring of 1963 the Deputy Under Secretary of State claimed that 30,000 casualties had been inflicted on the Viet Cong in 1962—a figure twice as large as the estimated size of the Viet Cong forces at the beginning of the year. So the Chairman of the Joint Chiefs of Staff could say in May 1965, "More than 50,000 South Vietnamese soldiers have been killed or wounded in battle since 1960," and the Secretary of State could say six weeks later, "From 1961 to the present . . . South Vietnamese armed forces have lost some 25,000 dead and 51,000 wounded"—a splendid increase of 50 per cent in a remarkably short time.

The figures on enemy strength are totally baffling, at least to the ordinary citizen relying on the daily newspaper. Thus President Johnson on April 4, 1966, said that 50,000 of the enemy had been killed since the beginning of the year. Four months later, the *New York Times,* on August 10, said that "according to official figures" the enemy had suffered 31,571 killed in action since January 1—a startling decline of 20,000 in the number of enemy deaths from President Johnson's April figure. The *Times* added, citing "the latest intelligence reports" in Saigon, that the number of enemy troops in South Vietnam had nevertheless increased 52,000 since January 1, to a total of 282,000. The infiltration estimate ranged from 35,000 as "definite" to 54,000 as "probably." If these figures mean anything, they suggest that the Viet Cong picked up from 30,000 to 50,000 local recruits in this period—a possibility which casts doubt on our incessant reports about the steady decline of Viet Cong morale.

Even the rather vital problem of how many North Vietnamese troops are in South Vietnam is swathed in mystery. The *Times* reported on August 7, 1966: "About 40,000 North Vietnamese troops are believed by allied intelligence to be in the South." According to an Associated Press dispatch from Saigon printed in the *Christian Science Monitor* of August 15:

> The South Vietnamese Government says 102,500 North Vietnamese combat troops and support battalions have infiltrated into South Vietnam.

These figures are far in excess of United States intelligence estimates, which put the maximum number of North Vietnamese in the South at about 54,000.

But General Westmoreland told his Texas press conference on August 14 that the enemy force included "about 110,000 main-force North Vietnamese regular army troops." Then in the *U.S. News & World Report* three months later (November 28, 1966) the following exchange took place:

Q: How many North Vietnamese regulars do you figure there are in the South?
Westmoreland: Approximately 50,000.

The General neglected to explain what had happened to the extra 60,000 he had reported in August (and, needless to say, *U.S. News* did not ask him). Yet the American press continues solemnly to print such figures as if they meant something. Richard Goodwin has cogently summed up the condition of our statistics: "If we take the number of enemy we are supposed to be killing, add to that the defectors, along with a number of wounded much less than our own ratio of wounded to killed, we find we are wiping out the entire North Vietnamese force every year. This truly makes their continued resistance one of the marvels of the world."

Nor is our ignorance confined to battle-order statistics. An inordinate optimism has marked nearly all official statements about Vietnam since 1950—an optimism always discredited by events but somehow rarely discrediting the optimists, who continue to be heard reverently by the Congress and the press. We have been constantly told of our steady progress in pushing back the enemy; yet in bitter fact hardly more of the countryside of South Vietnam was 'secure' in 1966 than in 1965 or 1964. "In the main, and at the time that it matters most," as Philip Geyelin put it in the *Wall Street Journal* after a visit to Vietnam, "the decision-makers don't really know what they are talking about." The sad truth is that our government just doesn't know a lot of things it pretends to know. It is not discreditable that it should know them, for the facts are elusive and the judgments incredibly difficult. But it is surely inexcusable that it should pretend to know things it does not —and that it should commit the nation to a policy involving the greatest dangers on a foundation so vague and precarious. And it is even less excusable that it should pass its own ignorance on to the American people and to the world as certitude. "The air is charged with rhetoric," Richard Goodwin has written. ". . . Much of it is important and sincere and well-meaning. Some is intended to deceive. Some is deliberate lie and distortion. . . . With full allowance for necessary uncertainties I believe there has never been such intense and widespread deception and confusion as that which surrounds this war. The continual downpour of contradiction, misstatements and kaleidoscopically shifting attitudes has been so torrential that it has almost numbed the capacity to separate truth from conjecture and falsehood."

All this has produced what may, in the long run, be the most serious cost of all—a cost both domestic and foreign: the ebbing away of belief in the American government. It is an irony that a war undertaken to demonstrate the credibility of the American word should end in erosion of confidence in American integrity and purpose. When the Opinion Research Corporation conducted a poll of Western Europe in the autumn of 1966, asking under which President—Eisenhower, Kennedy or Johnson—American prestige had been greatest, the result was 74 per cent for Kennedy, 11 per cent for Eisenhower and 2 per cent for Johnson. The appearance of flim-flam, showmanship and manipulation in Washington has created a crisis of credibility from which it may take the nation a long time to recover.

VI

IS CHINA THE ENEMY IN VIETNAM?

So NOW WE ARE SET on the course of widening the war—even at the cost of multiplying American casualties in Vietnam and deepening American troubles at home and abroad; even at the risk of miring our nation in a hopeless and endless conflict on the mainland of Asia beyond the effective employment of our national power and beyond the range of our primary interests; even with the loss of national credibility and at the hazard of nuclear war.

Why does the administration feel that these costs must be paid and these risks run? Hovering behind our policy is a larger idea—the idea that the war in Vietnam is not just a local conflict between Vietnamese but a fateful test of wills between China and the United States.

Our political and rhetorical escalation of the war has been almost as perilous as our military escalation. President Kennedy's effort was to pull Laos out of the context of great-power conflict and reduce the civil war there to rational proportions. As he told Khrushchev at Vienna in 1961, Laos was just not important enough to entangle two great nations. President Johnson, on the other hand, has systematically inflated the significance of the war in Vietnam. It is, he has said, "a contest as far-reaching and as vital as any we have ever waged."

The reason for this, it appears, is China. On December 23, 1964, the Secretary of State told his press conference—as reported the next day by Chalmers Roberts of the *Washington Post*—"that the loss of Vietnam would mean that the Red Chinese 'primitive, militant doctrine of world revolution' would not stop with the conquest of Vietnam. 'I should think,' he said, 'they would simply move the problem to the next country and the next and the next.' . . . This problem will continue, he said, until the Red Chinese decide 'to leave their neighbors alone and not to press militantly their notion of world revolution.' " "We have tried to make it clear over and over again," the Secretary of State put it to the Senate Foreign Relations Committee, "that although Hanoi is the prime actor in this situation, that it is the policy of Peking that has greatly stimulated Hanoi. . . . It is Ho Chi Minh's war. Maybe it is Mao Tse-tung's war." The object of our policy, according to the Under Secretary of State, is to "prevent Red China from establishing its hegemony over the East Asian land mass." "In the forties and fifties," according to President Johnson, "we took our stand in Europe to protect the freedom of those threatened by aggression. Now the center of attention has shifted to another part of the world where aggression is on the march. Our stand must be as firm as ever." Given this view—the view, as well summarized by U Thant, that "the conflict is a kind of holy war between two powerful political ideologies"—it is presumably necessary to pay the greatest costs and run the greatest risks—or else invite the greatest defeat.

Given this view, too, there is no reason not to Americanize the war. President Kennedy did not believe that the war in Vietnam could succeed as a war of white men against Asians. We have now junked this doctrine. Instead, we have enlarged our military presence until it is the only thing that matters in South Vietnam, and we plan now to make it still larger; we have summoned the

Saigon leaders, like tribal chieftains on a retainer, to a conference in an American state; we crowd the streets of Saigon with American generals (fifty-eight at last count) and visiting stateside dignitaries. In short, we have seized every opportunity to make clear to the world that this is an *American* war—and, in doing this, we have surely gone far to make the war unwinnable.

The proposition that our real enemy in Vietnam is China is basic to the policy of widening the war. It is the vital element in the administration case. Yet the proof our leaders have adduced has been exceedingly sketchy and almost perfunctory. The American government, indeed, acts as if the proposition were so self-evident that it requires no demonstration—in spite of the fact that the countries most directly threatened by Chinese expansion, Russia, Japan and India, apparently do not accept it. If pressed, our government offers proof by ideology or proof by analogy. It does not offer proof by reasoned argument or by concrete illustration.

The proof by ideology has relied on the syllogism that the Viet Cong, North Vietnam and China are all communist states and *therefore* must be part of the same conspiracy, and that, since the Viet Cong are the weakest of the three and China is the strongest, the Viet Cong must *therefore* be the spearhead of a coordinated Chinese plan of expansion. The clichés about a centralized communist conspiracy aiming at monolithic world revolution are still cherished in the State Department, in spite of what has struck lay observers as a rather evident fragmentation of the communist world. Thus, as late as May 9, 1965, after half a dozen years of vociferous Russo-Chinese quarreling, Thomas C. Mann, then No. 3 man in the Department, could babble about "instruments of Sino-Soviet power" and "orders from the Sino-Soviet military bloc." As late as January 28, 1966, the Secretary of State was still running on about "their world revolution," and again, on February 18, about "the Communists" and their "larger design."

While the department may have finally accepted the

reality of the Russo-Chinese schism, it still does not grasp the larger implications of the shattering of communist universalism. For this schism has done a good deal more than simply to divide Russia and China: what it has done is to set all communist states free to pursue national policies. It has thereby transformed the character of the communist problem. For, in an age of centralized communist control, the extension of communism did mean the pretty automatic extension of Russian power. In the thirties or forties, if the communists took over a country, the result was to heighten the threat to the security of the democratic world. But in the age of polycentrism the extension of communism no longer means an automatic extension of Russian, or of Chinese, power. All it may mean is that a country has succumbed to a dismal and dogmatic creed, with subsequent repression for its people and losses for foreign investors; and such a development, however deplorable, does not *per se* create a deadly strategic threat to the security of the democracies.

The crucial fact is that in a world without a clear center of communist authority—and especially in countries where communism can survive only as it becomes a nationalist movement—we can no longer assume that every communist state will be a puppet or, in the lingo of Senator Dodd, a 'slave state.'[1] On the contrary we must expect communist states to begin to act like other independent countries. This does not mean that we can necessarily look to the multiplication of Yugoslavias—

---

[1] Those whose passion it is to eliminate Communist China as a world power must some day ask themselves whether it is really to the interest of the United States to restore Moscow as the sole and single center of communist authority and thereby assist the Soviet Union to rebuild the relatively centralized and unified international communist movement of the thirties and forties. Our natural preference for the Soviet Union in its doctrinal disputes with China should not blind us to the fact that the national interests of the Soviet Union may well be more in direct conflict than those of China with the national interests of the United States.

i.e., of communist nations eager to get on good terms with the west—but we can probably look to the multiplication of Rumanias—i.e., of communist nations still deeply anti-American but determined to recover control over their own polities and to assert their independence of Moscow and Peking.

The mere fact a state proclaims itself communist is thus no longer by that fact itself proof that it will serve as the obedient instrument of expanding Russian or Chinese power. The abstraction no longer settles the question. What is required is specific demonstration in each particular case. Yet the State Department (I speak of the institution; many individuals, of course, wholly understand the implications of life in the polycentrist world) continues indolently in the old course, treating Asian communism as if it were a homogeneous system of aggression. The premise of our Vietnam policy has been that the Viet Cong equal Hanoi and Hanoi equals Peking.

Obviously the Viet Cong, Hanoi and Peking have interests in common and strong ideological affinities. Obviously, Peking would rejoice in a Hanoi-Viet Cong victory. But they also have divergent interests and purposes—and the divergencies may prove in the end to be stronger than the affinities. Recent developments in North Korea are instructive. If any country was bound to Peking by ties of gratitude, it was North Korea, which was preserved as an independent state by Chinese intervention fifteen years ago. If any country today is at the mercy of Peking, it is again North Korea. When North Korea now declares in vigorous language its independence of China, does anyone suppose that North Vietnam, imbued with historic mistrust of China and led by that veteran Russian agent, Ho Chi Minh, will be more reliable and slavish in subservience to Peking?

The other part of the administration case has been proof by analogy, especially the good old Munich analogy. "I'm not the village idiot," the Secretary of State recently confided to Stewart Alsop. "I know Hitler was an Austrian and Mao is Chinese. . . . But what is common between the two situations is the phenomenon of aggression." The Secretary of State had even the imagination to suggest that an exhortation to the underdeveloped world delivered in 1965 by the Chinese Defense Minister, Marshal Lin Piao, was a blueprint for world conquest comparable to Hitler's *Mein Kampf*.

The chosen technique for Chinese expansion, according to the American government, is the 'war of national liberation'—a mellifluous phrase which the Daughters of the American Revolution should not perhaps have surrendered so readily to the Communists. The Vietnam war, President Johnson told the American Legion, "is meant to be the opening salvo in a series of bombardments or, as they are called in Peking, 'wars of liberation.'" If this technique works this week in Vietnam, the administration suggests, it will be tried next week in Uganda and Peru. But, if it is defeated in Vietnam, the Chinese will know that we will not let it succeed elsewhere. "What happens in South Vietnam," the President cried at Omaha, "will determine—yes, it will determine—whether ambitious and aggressive nations can use guerrilla warfare to conquer their weaker neighbors."

One thing is sure about the Vietnam riddle: it will not be solved by bad historical analogies. It seems a trifle forced, for example, to equate a civil war in what was for centuries the entity of Vietnam (Marshal Ky, after all, is a North Vietnamese himself[2] and Pham Van Dong, the premier of North Vietnam, is from the south) with Hitler's invasion of Czechoslovakia across old and well-established lines of national division.

When President Eisenhower invoked the Munich analogy in 1954 in an effort to involve the British in Indochina, Prime Minister Churchill, a pretty keen

---

[2] Ky's effort to pack the Saigon government with other North Vietnamese caused a cabinet crisis in the last months of 1966. Yet the American officials continue to talk as if North and South Vietnam were entirely distinct national states.

student of Munich in his day, was unmoved. He evidently saw no useful parallel between Hitler, the man on the bicycle who could not stop, a madman commanding vast military force and requiring immediate and visible success, and the ragged bands and limited goals of Ho Chi Minh. Nor evidently could he see any useful parallel between Europe—a developed continent with well-defined national frontiers, interests and identities and a highly organized equilibrium of power—and Southeast Asia, an underdeveloped subcontinent filled with fictitious states in vague, chaotic, and unpredictable revolutionary ferment. And, if Mao rather than Ho is the Asian Hitler, even the Chinese have neither the overwhelmingly military power nor the timetable of aggression nor, apparently, the pent-up mania for instant expansion which would justify the parallel. As for the Lin Piao document, the Rand Corporation, which evidently read it with more care than the State Department bothered to do, concluded that, far from being Mao's *Mein Kampf,* it was a message to the Viet Cong that they could win "only if they rely primarily on their own resources and their own revolutionary spirit," and that it revealed "the lack, rather than the extent, of Peking's past and present control over Hanoi's actions."

In any case, guerrilla warfare is not a tactic to be mechanically applied by central headquarters to faraway countries. More than any other form of warfare, it is dependent on conditions and opportunities within the countries themselves. Defeating communist guerrillas in Greece, the Philippines, Malaya and Venezuela—defeating communist aggression in Korea—did not prevent guerrilla warfare in Vietnam. Whether there are wars of national liberation in Uganda and Peru will depend, not on what happens in Vietnam, but on what happens in Uganda and Peru.

Nor need we exaggerate the inevitability of communist takeovers of nationalist revolutions. We have been hypnotized by the notion that, when a revolution begins in an underdeveloped country, the Communists are bound to win out. But history shows this to be the exception, not the rule. "It would be a gross oversimplification," Secretary McNamara has reminded us, "to regard Communism as the central factor in every conflict throughout the underdeveloped world. Of the 149 serious insurgencies in the past eight years, Communists have been involved in only 58 of them—38 per cent of the total—and this includes seven in which a Communist regime itself was the target of the uprising." Communist strength in underdeveloped countries is ordinarily in the cities, the universities, the trade unions, not in the hills—and, where Communists wish to penetrate the normal political and institutional life of a country, there is no quicker way to destroy their prospects than by a resort to violence: cf. Indonesia and Venezuela.

One may look at Algeria, for example, or Egypt, or the countries of Black Africa, or Bolivia, or Indonesia; all these states have undergone drastic upheavals, and their nationalism has taken ardent and aggressive forms. Often these upheavals have produced regimes which do not much like the west or the United States. But the new nationalist regimes typically do not much like communism either. The striking fact of the post-war years is surely the failure of the communists to ride to power on nationalist upheavals—in short, the failure of the "war of national liberation" as a communist tactic. Where the communists have won out, as in China and North Vietnam, it is because they were able to place themselves at the head of nationalist movements during the Second World War. (The other major communist post-war success—Cuba—is a special case; Castro made his own revolution and then personally carried it into the communist empire.)

Certainly the containment of China will be a major problem for the next generation. But let us not confuse the prevention of Chinese aggression with the suppression of nationalist revolution. The containment of national communism in the polycentrist sixties will be very different from the containment of international communism in the monolithic forties. The record thus far suggests that the force most likely to contain Chinese expansionism in Asia (and Africa, too) will be not American intervention but local nationalism (plus the dogmatism and folly which have thus far made China such a hopeless washout as a revolutionary power and have alienated every Communist Party in the East except for New Zealand). Sometimes local nationalism may call on American support, but not always. Countries like Burma and Cambodia preserve their autonomy without American assistance.[3] The Africans have dealt with the Chinese on their own. The two heaviest blows recently suffered by Peking—the destruction of the Communist Party in Indonesia and the declaration of independence by North Korea—took place without benefit of American patronage or rhetoric.[4] Indeed, too overt American intervention may actually have the effect of smothering the forces of local nationalism or driving them to the other side and thereby ultimately weakening the containment of China.

In the unpredictable decades ahead, the most effective bulwark against an aggressive national communist state in some circumstances may well be national com-

[3] U Thant has observed of his native country: "The Burmese Communist Party is still underground after seventeen years and is still illegal. . . . Burma has over a thousand miles of land frontier with mainland China. If the Burmese Government had decided at some stage to seek outside military assistance . . . I am sure that Burma would have experienced one of two alternatives: either the country would be divided in two parts or the whole country would have become communist long ago." Or, in the words of Under Secretary Ball, "The people of Southeast Asia have, over the centuries, shown an obstinate insistence on shaping their own destiny which the Chinese have not been able to overcome."

[4] It is curiously argued that the Indonesian generals would not have resisted the Communist take-over had it not been for the American presence in Vietnam a thousand miles away. This proposition omits the fact that, if the generals had not resisted the take-over, they would all have been horribly killed. They were fighting for their lives.

munism in surrounding states. A rational policy of containing China could have recognized that a communist Vietnam under Ho might be a better instrument of containment than a shaky Saigon regime led by right-wing mandarins or air force generals. Had Ho taken over all Vietnam in 1954, he might today be soliciting Soviet support to strengthen his resistance to Chinese pressure, and this situation, however appalling for the people of South Vietnam, would obviously be better for the United States than the one in which we are floundering today. And now, alas, it may be almost too late: the whole thrust of United States policy since 1954, and more than ever since the bombing of the north began, has been not to pry Peking and Hanoi apart but to drive them together.

And now we are told that a higher obligation awaits us: that history has summoned America to be an Asian power—not just a Pacific power, which of course it has been since Commodore Perry opened up Japan, but a power with vital political interests and urgent military commitments on the mainland of Asia. The theory of the United States as an Asian power was the tacit point of President Johnson's Manila tour, as it has been the explicit point of Vice President Humphrey's eloquence about a Great Society for Asia. One cannot doubt the genuineness of the administration's belief that East Asia is manifest destiny's next stop.

Can Mr. Johnson and Mr. Humphrey, two astute and experienced men, really be serious about this? Evidently they are; and their Asian vision is not dishonorable. It derives from the psyche of Franklin Roosevelt rather than Theodore—from the desire, as they represent it to themselves, not to aggrandize the power of America but to help Asians become more like Americans. It is a form of imperialism unknown to Lenin: sentimental imperialism. Not perhaps unknown to Kipling: the white man's burden. This is what they mean—and they mean it decently.

But do they mean it sensibly? One can argue, I think,

that the United States could embark on no more preposterous adventure in the seventh decade of the twentieth century than the salvation of Asia. This undertaking, in the first place, ignores the central historic transformation of this century—the emergence of Asia as an equal force on the world scene, which has led to the recovery by Asians of their ancient sense of ineffable superiority to the western barbarians. As long ago as 1954, when Christopher Mayhew of England suggested to Ho Chi Minh that the west had a peace-keeping role in Asia, Ho replied sardonically, "Suppose we Vietnamese—together perhaps with the Indians—proposed ourselves for a peace-keeping role in Europe. What would you Europeans think?" What indeed? How can the west continue to suppose that it can assign itself a role in Asia which Asia cannot claim in Europe or America? Nor can President Johnson really suppose that the support at the Manila Conference of four American dependencies in Asia—South Vietnam, South Korea, Thailand and the Philippines, with a total population of 103 million—offers the United States a firm moral, political or military basis for intervention.

It must be argued, moreover, that the conception of the United States as an Asian power violates the logic of our own history. For history prescribes two tables of priorities for the United States—one based on strategic significance, the other on cultural accessibility. And by both standards Western Europe and Latin America are the parts of the world which matter most to the United States. We could survive the subjection of Asia, Africa, the Middle East, Eastern Europe or Polynesia by a hostile power or ideology; but, if either Western Europe or Latin America were organized against North America, our position would be parlous indeed. And Western Europe and Latin America are the parts of the world to which a common intellectual tradition gives us a hope of reciprocal understanding.

We express our daily concern about the underdeveloped world. But the one part of the underdeveloped world which is western in its institutions and values—and the one part of the western world which is underdeveloped—is Latin America. If we cannot relate ourselves to the democratic development of Latin America, if we cannot, as President Kennedy said in the speech launching the Alliance for Progress, demonstrate here "that man's unsatisfied aspiration for economic progress and social justice can best be achieved by free men working within a framework of democratic institutions," how can we ever suppose that we can advance the cause of democracy in the alien, mysterious and impenetrable cultures of Asia and Africa? Yet Latin America falls to the end of the queue, while all energy and concern are absorbed by Vietnam.

Expansive rhetoric is the occupational disease of national leaders. But serious leaders preserve a relationship, however tenuous, between rhetoric and reality. One cannot remember a more complete dissociation between words and responsibility than in the United States government today: official speeches are always manipulative in part, but now they are almost nothing else. The dedication of the United States to the salvation of Asia represents a translation of rhetorical extravagance into national policy. The President of the United States can hardly understand the eastern seaboard of his own country; why in the world does he think he can understand the eastern seaboard of Asia? If meant seriously, the idea of a Great Society for Asia is surely a fantastic overcommitment of American thought and resources. If meant as a rhetorical flourish, it is frivolity. However meant, the proposition demands a most rigorous and thoughtful assessment of the limits and possibilities of America's role in the world. It demands the confrontation of an issue deep in the historical consciousness of the United States: whether this country is a chosen people, uniquely righteous and wise, with a moral mission to all mankind; or whether it is one of many nations in a multifarious world, endowed with traditions and purposes, legitimate but not infallible, as other nations have legitimate and fallible traditions and purposes of their own, and committed not to an American century but to what President Kennedy used to call a world of diversity—"a robust and vital world community, founded on nations secure in their own independence, and united by allegiance to world peace." The ultimate choice is between messianism and maturity.

The argument that the United States and China must be locked in mortal combat on the mainland of Asia is not an observation but a prophecy, even if a prophecy which masquerades as historical analogy. It therefore raises larger questions about the way statesmen use history—or are used by it.

VII

THE INSCRUTABILITY OF HISTORY

*A*S ONE who is by profession an historian and has been by occasion a government official, I have long been fascinated and perplexed by the interaction between history and public decision: fascinated because, by this process, past history becomes an active partner in the making of new history; perplexed because the role of history in this partnership remains both elusive and tricky.

It is elusive because, if one excludes charismatic politics—the politics of the prophet and the medicine man—one is bound to conclude that all thought which leads to decisions of public policy is in essence historical. Public decision in rational politics necessarily implies a guess about the future derived from the experience of the past. It implies an expectation, or at the very least a hope, that certain actions will produce tomorrow the same sort of results they produced yesterday. This guess about the future may be based on a comprehensive theory of historical change, as with the Marxists; or it may be based on specific analogies drawn from the past; or it may be based on an unstated and intuitive sense of the way things happen. But, whatever it is based on, it involves, explicitly or implicitly, an historical judgment.

And the problem is tricky because, when explicit historical judgments intervene, one immediately encounters a question which is, in the abstract, insoluble: Is the history invoked really the source of policies, or is it the source of arguments designed to vindicate policies adopted for antecedent reasons? Moreover, even when history is in some sense the source of policies, the lessons of history are generally so ambiguous that the antecedent reasons often determine the choice between alternative historical interpretations. Thus, in France between the wars Reynaud and Mandel drew one set of conclusions from the First World War, Bonnet and Laval another. Yet one cannot, on the other hand, reduce the function of history in public policy to that of mere rationalization, for historical models acquire a life of their own. Once a statesman begins to identify the present with the past, he may in time be carried further than he intends by the bewitchment of analogy.

However hard it may be to define with precision the role of history in public policy, it is evident that this role must stand or fall on the success of history as a means of prediction—on the proposition that knowledge of yesterday provides guidance for tomorrow. This is a point, it should immediately be said, on which professional historians, on the whole, have few illusions among themselves. They privately regard history as its own reward; they study it for the intellectual and aesthetic fulfillment they find in the disciplined attempt to reconstruct the past and, perhaps, for the ironic aftertaste in the contemplation of man's heroism and folly, but for no more utilitarian reason. They understand better than outsiders that historical training confers no automatic wisdom in the realm of public affairs. Guizot, Bancroft, Macaulay, Thiers, Morley, Bryce, Theodore Roosevelt, Woodrow Wilson: one cannot say that their training as historians deeply influenced their practice as politicians; and the greatest of them—Roosevelt and Wilson—were harmed as politicians by exactly the moralism from which the study of history might have saved them. But then neither was a particularly good historian.[1]

Yet historians, in spite of their candor within the fellowship, sometimes invoke arguments of a statelier sort in justifying themselves to society. Thus Raleigh: "We may gather out of History a policy no less wise than eternal; by the comparison and application of other men's fore-passed miseries with our own errours and ill-deservings." Or Burke: "In history, a great volume is unrolled for our instruction, drawing the materials of future wisdom from the past errors and infirmities of mankind." In what sense is this true? Why should history help us foresee the future? Because presumably history repeats itself enough to make possible a range of historical generalization; and because generalization, sufficiently multiplied and interlaced, can generate insight into the shape of things to come.

Many professional historians—perhaps most—reject the idea that generalization is the goal of history. We all respond, in Marc Bloch's phrase, to "the thrill of learning singular things." Indeed, it is the commitment to concrete reconstruction as against abstract generalization—to life as against laws—which distinguishes history from sociology. Yet, on the other hand, as Crane Brinton once put it, "the doctrine of the absolute uniqueness of events in history seems nonsense." Even historians who are skeptical of attempts to discern a final and systematic order in history acknowledge the existence of a variety of uniformities and recurrences. There can be no question that generalizations about the past, defective as they may be, are possible—and that they can strengthen the capacity of statesmen to deal with the future.

So historians have long since identified a life-cycle

---

[1] Churchill is a different matter; but he was a politician who turned to history, not an historian who turned to politics. So too was Kennedy.

of revolution which, if properly apprehended, might have spared us misconceptions about the Russian Revolution—first, about its goodwill and, later, when we abandoned belief in its goodwill, about the fixity and permanence of its fanatical purpose—and which, if consulted today, might save us from the notion that the Chinese Revolution will be forever cast in its present mold. Historical generalizations in a number of areas— the processes of economic development, for example, or the impact of industrialization and urbanization, or the effect of population growth, or the influence of climate or sea power or the frontier, or the circulation of political elites or entrepreneurial innovation—will enlarge the wisdom of the statesman, giving his responses to the crises of the moment perspective, depth and an instinct for the direction and flow of events. The consequences for American society of the frustrations generated by limited war—the McCarthyism effect—is probably an example of permissible generalization. Sometimes this wisdom may even lead to what Bloch called "the paradox of prevision"—to the point when men, sufficiently warned by historical extrapolation of horrid eventualities, may take action to avert them, which means that prevision may be destroyed by prevision.

The result is historical insight: that is, a sense of what is possible and probable in human affairs, derived from a feeling for the continuities and discontinuities of existence. This sense is comparable not to the mathematical equations of the physicist but to the diagnostic judgments of the doctor. It is this form of historical insight which has led in recent years to Bertrand de Jouvenel's *L'Art de la Conjecture* and to the stimulating intellectual exercise involved in the search for *futuribles*. But *futuribles* are speculative constructions of possible long-range futures, useful perhaps to those who may be presidents and prime ministers in 2000, hardly to their predecessors in 1970.

Still every day around the planet great decisions are being made (or at least rationalized) in terms of short-run historical estimates. The whole Marxist world, of course, is sworn to a determinist view of the future, according to which fixed causes produce fixed effects and mankind is moving along a predestined path through predestined stages to a single predestined conclusion. For the Marxists, history has become a 'positive model': it prescribes not only for the long but for the short run, not only strategy but tactics—the immediate policies to be favored, courses pursued, action taken. It is a tribute to the devotion of Marxists, if hardly to their intelligence, that they have remained so indefatigably loyal to their metaphysic in spite of the demonstrated limits of Marxism as a system of prediction.

For, if any thesis was central to the Marxist vision of history, it was that the process of modernization, of industrialization, of social and economic development, would infallibly carry every nation from feudalism through capitalism to communism: that the communist society was the inevitable culmination of the development process. Thus Marx contended that, the more developed a country was, the more prepared it was for communism, and that communism in consequence must come first to the most industrialized nations. In fact, communism has come only to nations in a relatively early stage of development, like Russia and China, and it has come to such nations precisely as a means to modernization, not as a consequence of it. Instead of being the climax of the development process, the end of the journey, communism is now revealed as a technique of social discipline which a few countries in early stages of development have adopted in the hope of speeding the pace of modernization. Instead of the ultimate destinations toward which all societies are ineluctably moving, communism now appears an epiphenomenon of the transition from stagnation to development. Modernization, as it proceeds, evidently carries nations not toward Marx but away from Marx—and this would appear true even of the Soviet Union itself.

History thus far has refuted the central proposition

in Marx's system of prediction. It has also refuted important corollary theses—notably the idea that the free economic order could not possibly last. Far from obeying dogma and perishing of its own inner contradictions, free society in the developed world has rarely displayed more creativity and vitality. It is casting as powerful a spell on the intellectuals and the youth of the communist world as the communist world cast on us during the Depression thirty years ago.

Why did Marx go wrong here? His forecast of the inevitable disintegration of free society was plausibly based on the *laissez faire* capitalism of the mid-nineteenth century. This devil-take-the-hindmost economic order did very likely contain the seeds of its own destruction—especially in those tendencies, pronounced irreversible by Marx, toward an ever widening gap between rich and poor (alleged to guarantee the ultimate impoverishment of the masses) and toward an ever increasing frequency and severity of structural economic crisis (alleged to guarantee the progressive instability of the system). This may indeed be a salient example of the "paradox of prevision"; for the Marxist forecast unquestionably stimulated progressive democrats to begin the reform of classical capitalism through the invention of the affirmative state. "The more we condemn unadulterated Marxian Socialism," Theodore Roosevelt used to say, "the stouter should be our insistence on thoroughgoing social reforms." The combination of the affirmative state with the extraordinary success of the free economic order as an engine of production—a success which, contrary to *laissez faire* dogma, government intervention increased rather than hampered—eventually thwarted the Marxist prophecy.

In the end, the Marxists were undone by Marxism. Ideology told them that those who owned the economy *must* own the state, and the state could therefore never act against their desires or interests. Yet fifteen years before the *Communist Manifesto* an American President, Andrew Jackson, had already suggested that the state in a democratic society, far from being the instrument of the possessors, could well become the means by which those whom Jackson called the "humble members of society" might begin to redress the balance of social power against those whom Hamilton had called the "rich and well-born." Thus, in the twentieth-century developed world, the economic machine drowned the revolution in consumers' goods, while the affirmative state, with its policies of piece-meal intervention in the economy, brought about both a relative redistribution of wealth (defeating Marx's prediction of the immiseration of the poor) and a relative stabilization of the economy (defeating Marx's prediction of ever deepening cyclical crisis). The last place to look for a Marxist victory is precisely the place where Marx said it would come first—i.e., in the most developed countries.

So the Marxist prophecy of a single obligatory destiny for mankind has missed in both its parts: in its prediction of the irresistible breakdown of the free economy, and in its prediction of the irresistible triumph of communism as the fulfillment of the development process. In spite of many subsidiary insights and successes, Marxism must surely stand in our time as the spectacular flop of history as prophecy. The failure, indeed, has been so complete that contemporary Marxists revile each other in seeking the true meaning of the most elementary doctrines; the more fanatical stand Marx on his head, rejecting his basic theory and arguing that communism will come "out of the countryside," not the city.

Yet the democratic world is hardly in a position to take too much satisfaction from the intellectual collapse of Marxism. It is true that our philosophical heritage— empirical, pragmatic, ironic, pluralistic, competitive— has happily inoculated us against rigid, all-encompassing, absolute systems of historical interpretation. But, though we may reject the view of history as metaphysically set and settled, we seem at times to embrace our own forms of historical fatalism, even if we invoke history less as theology than as analogy. This is only a marginal advantage. The argument by metaphor can generate a certitude almost as mischievous as the argument by determinism.

For democratic policy-makers, history generally appears as a 'negative' rather than a 'positive' model. It instructs us, not like Marxism, in the things we must do, but in the things we must *not* do—unless we wish to repeat the mistakes of our ancestors. The traumatic experience of the First World War thus dominated the diplomacy of the Second World War, at least as far as the United States was concerned. So the American insistence on the doctrine of "unconditional surrender" in 1943 sprang from the belief that the failure to get unconditional surrender in 1918 had made possible the stab-in-the-back myth and guaranteed the revival of German nationalism. The American obsession with the United Nations came from the conviction that the failure to join the League of Nations had opened the way to the Second World War. The American readiness to make concessions to the Soviet Union (as Professor E. R. May has suggested) was based, in part, on an analogy with Clemenceau's France. The American President viewed the Soviet Union as a nation which, having lived in permanent insecurity, could be expected, like France twenty-five years earlier, to value security above almost anything else. "Roosevelt," Professor May has perceptively written, "was determined to see Stalin's point of view as Wilson had not seen Clemenceau's. He was determined that, in so far as possible, the Soviet Union should have the guarantees it wanted and should not be forced into the sullen self-preoccupation of the France of Poincaré."

The Second World War, then, provided a new traumatic experience. In the years since, the consciousness of policymakers has been haunted by the Munich and Yalta analogies—the generalization, drawn from attempts to accommodate Hitler in 1938, and Stalin in 1945, that appeasement always assures new aggression.

Of these analogies, Munich, as the more lucid in its pattern and the more emphatic in its consequence, has been the more powerful; Yalta figures rather as a complicated special case. I trust that a graduate student some day will write a doctoral essay on the influence of the Munich analogy on the subsequent history of the twentieth century. Perhaps in the end he will conclude that the multitude of errors committed in the name of "Munich" may exceed the original error of 1938.

Certainly Munich was a tragic mistake, and its lesson was that the appeasement of a highly wound-up and heavily armed totalitarian state in the context of a relatively firm and articulated continental equilibrium of power was likely to upset the balance and make further aggression inevitable. But to conclude from this that all attempts to avert war by negotiation must always be 'Munichs' goes beyond the evidence. No one understood this better than the greatest contemporary critic of Munich. An historian himself, Winston Churchill well understood the limits of historical analogy. So he defined the issue in his chapter on Munich in *The Gathering Storm*:

> It may be well here to set down some principles of morals and action which may be a guide in the future. No case of this kind can be judged apart from its circumstances. . . .
>
> Those who are prone by temperament and character to seek sharp and clear-cut solutions of difficult and obscure problems, who are ready to fight whenever some challenge comes from a foreign power, have not always been right. On the other hand, those whose inclination is to bow their heads, to seek patiently and faithfully for peaceful compromise, are not always wrong. On the contrary, in the majority of instances, they may be right, not only morally but from a practical standpoint. . . .
>
> How many wars have been precipitated by firebrands! How many misunderstandings which led to war could have been removed by temporising! How often

have countries fought cruel wars and then after a few years of peace found themselves not only friends but allies!

Sixteen years after Munich, when President Eisenhower invoked the Munich analogy to persuade the British to join the Americans in backing the French in Indochina, Churchill, as we have seen, was unimpressed. He rejected Eisenhower's analogy, which did not, of course, prevent Churchill's successor as prime minister two years later from seeing Nasser and the Middle East in terms of 1938 and committing his nation to the Suez adventure. This time it was Eisenhower who rejected the Munich analogy. Such incidents illustrate the depressing persistence of the mentality which makes policy through stereotype, through historical generalization wrenched illegitimately out of the past and imposed mechanically on the future. Santayana's aphorism must be reversed: too often it is those who *can* remember the past who are condemned to repeat it.

"No case of this kind," Churchill said, "can be judged apart from its circumstances." I well remember President Kennedy after the Cuban missile crisis in 1962 privately expressing his fear that people would conclude from his victory that all we would have to do thereafter in dealing with the Communists was to be tough and they would collapse. The missile crisis, he pointed out, had three distinctive features: it took place in an area where we enjoyed local conventional superiority, where Soviet national security was not directly engaged, and where the Russians lacked a case which they could convincingly sustain before the world. Things would be different, he said, if the situation were one where the Communists had the local superiority, where their national security was directly engaged, and where they could persuade themselves and others they were in the right.

Kennedy, who, like Churchill, had the mind of a first-class historian, was without illusion about the infallibility of historical analogy. The point is not terribly complicated. Burke long ago warned against the practice of viewing an object "as it stands stripped of every relation, in all the nakedness and solitude of metaphysical abstraction. Circumstances (which with some gentlemen pass for nothing) give in reality to every political principle its distinguishing color and discriminating effect." Even Toynbee, the magician of historical analogy, has remarked that historians are

> never in a position to guarantee that the entities which we are bringing into comparison are properly comparable for the purpose of our investigation. . . . However far we may succeed in going in our search for sets of identical examples on either side, we shall never be able to prove that there is not some non-identical factor that we have overlooked, and this non-identical factor is not the decisive factor that accounts for the different outcomes in different cases of what has looked to us like an identical situation but may not have been this in truth.

Or, as Mark Twain put it, somewhat more vividly, in *Following the Equator*: "We should be careful to get out of an experience only the wisdom that is in it—and stop there; lest we be like the cat that sits down on a hot stove lid. She will never sit down on a hot stove lid again—and that is well; but also she will never sit down on a cold one."

One cannot doubt that the study of history makes people wiser. But it is indispensable to understand the limits of historical analogy. Most useful historical generalizations are statements about massive social and intellectual movements over a considerable period of time. They make large-scale, long-term prediction possible. But they do not justify small-scale, short-term prediction. For short-run prediction is the prediction of detail and, given the complex structure of social events, the difficulty of anticipating the intersection or collision of different events and the irreducible mystery, if not invincible freedom, of individual decision, there are simply too many variables to warrant exact forecasts of the immediate future. History, in short, can answer questions, after a fashion, at long range. It cannot answer questions with confidence or certainty at short range. Alas, policy makers are rarely interested in the long run—"in the long run," as Keynes used to say, "we are all dead"—and the questions they put to history are thus most often the questions which history is least qualified to answer.

Far from offering a short cut to clairvoyance, history teaches us that the future is full of surprises and outwits all our certitudes. For the study of history issues not in scientific precision nor in moral finality but in irony. If twenty-five years ago, anyone had predicted that before the end of the decade of the forties Germany and Japan would be well on the way to becoming close friends and allies of Britain and the United States, he would have been considered mad. If fifteen years ago, as the Russians and Chinese were signing their thirty-year pact of amity and alliance, anyone predicted that by the end of the fifties they would be at each other's throats, he too would have been considered mad. The chastening fact is that many of the pivotal events of our age were unforeseen: from the Nazi-Soviet pact and the Tito-Stalin quarrel of years ago to such events in today's newspapers as the anti-communist upsurge in Indonesia and the overthrow of Nkrumah in Ghana (and his resurrection in Guinea).

Occasionally one reads in the American press that leading political figures in Washington are shaping their actions today by calculations with regard to the Democratic presidential nomination in 1972. I am sure that the men mentioned in such stories are themselves under no delusion about the hopelessness of such an undertaking. 1972 is as far away from 1966 as 1960 is, and no one reflecting on the unpredictability of the last six years in the United States could sensibly suppose that the next six are going to be any more predictable. I have often thought that a futurist trying to forecast the next three American Presidents in early 1940 would hardly have named as the first President after Franklin D. Roosevelt an obscure back-bench senator from Missouri, anticipating defeat by the governor of his state in the Democratic primaries; as the second, an unknown lieutenant-colonel in the United States Army; and, as the third, a kid still at college. Yet that sequence began to unfold in less time than between 1967 and 1972.

The salient fact about the historical process, so far as the short run is concerned, is its inscrutability. One must bear this in mind, I believe, when asked to accept drastic decisions now on the basis of someone's speculation as to what the behavior of Communist China will be a dozen years from now. In its coarsest form, this is the argument that "we must have a showdown with China before it gets the bomb." Here is the old preventive-war thesis we used to hear so often in the late forties: yet I do not think anyone can rationally contend that the world would be better off today had we dropped the bomb on Russia twenty years ago. Having been wrong so often in the past, how can we be sure we have achieved such infallibility now that we would risk the future of mankind on a guess?

Who can possibly predict with assurance that the Chinese Revolution will undertake the conquest of the world? The study of revolution has shown us that the emotional and doctrinal pitch of revolutions waxes and wanes; that, while revolutions at first may devour their children, in the end the children sometimes devour the revolutions; that even totalitarian revolutions fail at total mass indoctrination; that a successful revolution begins to develop a stake in the *status quo;* that post-revolutionary generations have their own identities and aspirations; that the possession of a major nuclear arsenal has thus far had a sobering effect on the possessor; that nations follow their historic interests rather more faithfully than they do their ideologies; and that there is no greater error than to try and deduce the policy of the future from the rhetoric of the present. Nor does the example of Hitler and *Mein Kampf* change this. Hitler was indeed the man on the bicycle; he had to keep moving. The Nazi revolution never got beyond the first messianic phase; its nature condemned it to *Götterdämmerung*. We must not forget that the Chinese revolutionary regime has already lasted five years longer than the whole life of the Third Reich. And we have seen in the case of the Soviet Union the permutation and erosion time and national interest have worked on what were once thought to be final motives and permanent objectives. With an equation so overflowing with variables, how can anyone forecast now the behavior of China twenty years from now?

History, in short, does not furnish the statesman with a detailed scenario of particular relationships or policies. Too often it equips his decisions with good rather than real reasons, holding out a mirror in which he fatuously sees his own face. This is not an argument against the knowledge of history: it is an argument against the superficial knowledge of history. The single analogy is never enough to penetrate a process so cunningly compounded not only of necessity but of contingency, fortuity, ignorance, stupidity and chance. The statesman who is surest that he can divine the future most urgently invites his own retribution. "The hardest strokes of heaven," Herbert Butterfield has written, "fall in history upon those who imagine that they can control things in a sovereign manner, playing providence not only for themselves but for the far future—reaching out into the future with the wrong kind of farsightedness, and gambling on a lot of risky calculations in which there must never be a single mistake."

The only antidote to a shallow knowledge of history is a deeper knowledge, the knowledge which produces not dogmatic certitude but diagnostic skill, not clairvoyance but insight. It offers the statesman a sense, at once, of short-run variables and long-run tendencies, and an instinct for the complexity of their intermingling, including the understanding that (as Rousseau once put it), "the ability to foresee that some things cannot be foreseen is a very necessary quality." Indeed, half the wisdom of statecraft, to borrow a phrase from Richard Goodwin, is "to leave as many options open as possible and decide as little as possible. . . . Since almost all important policy judgments are speculative, you must avoid risking too much on the conviction you are right."

Of course keeping too many options open too long may paralyze the lobe of decision and lose the game. There *does* come a time when accommodation turns into appeasement. This is the other half of the wisdom of statecraft: to accept the chronic obscurity of events without yielding, in Lincoln's words, firmness in the right as God gives us to see the right. In deciding when to decide, the criterion must be the human consequences —the results for people, not for doctrine.

Randolph Churchill's life of his father reproduces an extraordinary letter written seventy years ago by the young Winston Churchill to a New York politician of the time, Bourke Cockran. "The duty of government," Churchill said, "is to be first of all practical. I am for makeshifts and expediency. I would like to make the people who live on this world at the same time as I do better fed and happier generally. If incidentally I benefit posterity—so much the better—but I would not sacrifice my own generation to a principle however high or a truth however great."

Such an approach may seem too modest, even, perhaps, too cynical, for those theological statesmen whose self-righteousness has almost sunk our age. Most of these confident moralists have been high priests of one or another dogmatic faith (though some, alas, have been American Secretaries of State); but all have been prepared in the best conscience and in the name of history to sacrifice their generations on the altars of their own metaphors. It can only be said that, whether they see history as ideology or as analogy, they see it wrong. Far from unveiling the secret of things to come, history bestows a different gift: it makes us—or should make us —understand the extreme difficulty, the intellectual peril, the moral arrogance of supposing that the future will yield itself so easily to us.

"I returned," Ecclesiastes reminds us, "and saw under the sun that the race is not to the swift, nor the battle to the strong, neither yet bread to the wise nor riches to men of understanding, but time and chance happeneth to them all." The Old Testament carries the case against historical generalization to the extreme. But, without going so far, we can agree that history should lead statesmen to a profound and humbling sense of human frailty—to a recognition of the fact, so insistently demonstrated by experience and so tragically destructive of our most cherished certitudes, that the possibilities of history are far richer and more various than the human intellect is likely to conceive. This, and the final perception that while the tragedy of history implicates us all in the common plight of humanity, we are never relieved, despite the limits of our knowledge and the darkness of our understanding, from the necessity of meeting our obligations.

VIII

A MIDDLE COURSE

THE PROBLEM of balancing frailty and obligation is the essence of statecraft. Where does this problem leave us in Vietnam? For we have entered into obligations—not legal obligations under the SEATO treaty or to the succession of quasi-governments in Saigon, but moral obligations to those South Vietnamese who, under our encouragement and with the expectation of our support, have said and done things which will assure their imprisonment or death if the Viet Cong should take over South Vietnam by force. Yet the destruction of South Vietnam by the process of expanding the war is hardly a rational way to meet those obligations either. Are these the only alternatives: disorderly and humiliating withdrawal or enlarging the war?

Surely our statesmanship is not yet this bankrupt. I think a middle course is still possible if there were the will to pursue it. And this course must begin with a decision to stop widening and Americanizing the war— to limit our forces, actions, goals and rhetoric. Instead of bombing more places, sending in more troops, proclaiming ever more ardently that the fate of civilization will be settled in Vietnam, let us recover our cool and try to see the situation as it is: a horrid civil war in which communist guerrillas, enthusiastically aided and now substantially directed from Hanoi, are trying to establish a communist despotism in South Vietnam, not for the Chinese but for themselves. Let us understand that the ultimate problem here is not military but political. Let us adapt the means we employ to the end we seek.

Obviously, military action plays an indispensable role in the search for a political solution. Hanoi and the Viet Cong will not negotiate so long as they think they can win. Since stalemate is a self-evident precondition to negotiation, we must have enough American armed force in South Vietnam to leave no doubt in the minds of our adversaries that a communist government will not be imposed on South Vietnam by force. They must have no illusion about the prospect of an American withdrawal. The serious opposition to the escalation policy in the United States seeks not an American defeat but a negotiated settlement.

Therefore, holding the line in South Vietnam is essential. Surely, we already have enough American troops, firepower and installations in South Vietnam to make it clear that we cannot be beaten unless we choose to scuttle and run, which will not happen. The opponents of this strategy talk as if a holding action would put our forces under siege and relinquish all initiative to the enemy. This need not, of course, be so. It is possible to slow down a war without standing still; and, if our present generals can't figure out how to do this, then let us get generals who can. Generals Ridgway and Gavin could doubtless suggest some names. Moreover, there is a South Vietnamese army of some 600,000 men which can take all the initiative it wants. And if we are told that the South Vietnamese are unwilling or unable to fight the Viet Cong, whom they still greatly outnumber, then we must wonder all the more about the political side of the war.

The object of our military policy, as observers like

Henry Kissinger and James MacGregor Burns have proposed, should be the creation and stabilization of secure areas where the South Vietnamese might themselves undertake social and institutional development. Our resources should go, in the Vietnam jargon, more to clear-and-hold than to search-and-destroy (especially when search-and-destroy more often means search-and-drive-underground). We should stop the policy of hit-and-run raids, which drive the Viet Cong out of villages one day and permit them to slip back the next and resume their work of disruption and terror. And we should certainly get rid of those "one-star generals who," in the words of Sir Robert Thompson, "regard their tour in Vietnam as an opportunity to indulge in a year's big-game shooting from their helicopter howdahs at Government expense."

At the same time we should induce the Saigon government to institute generous amnesty provisions of the kind which worked so well in the Philippines. And we should further increase the incentive to come over by persuading the South Vietnamese to abandon the torture of prisoners, a practice not only horrible in itself but well calculated to make the enemy fight to the bitter end. In the meantime we must end our own shameful collaboration with this barbarism and stop turning Viet Cong prisoners over to the South Vietnamese when we know that torture is probable.

As for bombing the north, this has become a crucial issue in the strategy of negotiation. The Johnson administration regards bombing as the key to its "quotient of pain" policy. The argument is essentially that Hanoi is counting on the protest against the war within the United States to paralyze the American government and eventually to compel American withdrawal; that it will interpret concessions—such as a suspension of bombing —as evidence of weakness; and that the effect of concessions will therefore be to lead Hanoi to stiffen, not to moderate, its position. Thus in retrospect the thirty-seven-day bombing pause is regarded as an error. In a press conference in October 1966, when asked whether there would be a new bombing pause, the President replied, "I don't quite understand . . . why you want me to have our Marines and our airmen pause and put their hands behind their back while the other people don't pause and continue to shoot at them." Of course, no serious person has suggested that the United States should undertake a unilateral cease-fire; nor has any bombing pause been accompanied by a ban against war on the ground. But, press conference extravagance apart, a real fear remains that suspension would deter rather than hasten negotiation. The administration's conclusion is that only a hard line can force negotiation: keep up the pressure, bring in more men, step up the bombing, widen the war, until Hanoi and Peking come to their senses and stop molesting their neighbors. At some point increasing the "quotient of pain" will drive Hanoi to sue for peace.

Actually there is little reason to suppose that bombing will not continue to heighten Hanoi's resolve to fight on. The aerial war did not force the British to negotiation in 1940 nor the Germans in 1943-1945; nor, if America were being bombed today, would it produce in us anything but an absolute determination to win the war. Why do we expect the North Vietnamese to be greater cowards than we would be in like circumstance? And, as each new step in escalation fails to make much difference, the circle of targets under the "quotient of pain" policy will steadily widen—until what began as a policy of negotiation through escalation begins to turn imperceptibly into the policy which the administration has theoretically rejected: the pursuit of an illusory total military victory. Each new step, in addition, brings us closer to the point of Chinese or Russian participation in the war.

It is conceivable, moreover, to argue that there is little chance of negotiation at all so long as the bombing continues. "They will not come to the conference table on their knees," said Chester A. Ronning, who visited

Hanoi in June 1966 as a special envoy from the Canadian government; so long as the bombing continues, "there is not the slightest possibility of getting talks started." The theory that concession will be construed as weakness is far more persuasive when a country confronts another country of roughly its own strength— Britain against Germany in 1938, for example, or the United States against the Soviet Union in the 1940's, or possibly the United States against China at some future point; but surely not the United States against a small country whose total population is less than that of New York or California. Moreover, if Hanoi and the Viet Cong are to be denied their dream of taking over South Vietnam, they need some concessions to save the well-known oriental face: this is a truism of diplomacy. Beyond this, it is only realistic, if irritating, to recognize that our adversaries at this point simply do not take the word of the United States any more seriously than we take their word: once again the crisis of credibility. This is doubtless why Hanoi has put such stress on the withdrawal of American troops as a condition precedent to negotiation (though eventually this will have proved to be only a bargaining point); and this is why we will have to do something drastic and different before they begin to believe that we honestly want negotiation. Stopping the bombing seems the most likely thing. Nor does the failure of the pause of 1965-1966 refute any of these points. Thirty-seven days were hardly enough even to persuade our allies that we meant business, and left them no time to move on to the next and decisive stage—that is, trying to persuade Hanoi.

The bombing policy may have increased the inconvenience of infiltration, but it has also clearly increased its energy. General Westmoreland now tells us (November, 1966) that "for the last six months it's averaged more than 7000 a month." Without bombing it might have averaged 16,000; without bombing it might have averaged 2000: who can possibly tell? The only indisputable benefits from the bombing policy have come from the (transient) pleasure it has afforded the Saigon government and the American voter. Given its limited military and political results in North Vietnam, the gains in the domestic politics of South Vietnam and the United States are hardly important enough to justify a policy which probably makes negotiation impossible and certainly contains the risk of indefinite escalation into major war. The question is by no means easy; but, of possible military strategies, the strategy directed to the physical destruction of North Vietnam would seem on balance less likely to lead to negotiation than a strategy of determined long-run defense of South Vietnam. Let us therefore taper off the bombing of the north as prudently as we can.[1]

Even as we do this, it may take a long time before our adversaries are ready to negotiate in good faith. Indeed, Hanoi has shown no real interest in negotiation thus far except as a means of legalizing a Viet Cong victory. Ho Chi Minh, moreover, has substantial reasons for resisting negotiation, even in addition to his mistrust of the American word, to his hope that the Americans will get tired and go home and to the Chinese pressure on him to keep the war going. He has twice in the past entered into negotiation with the west—in 1946-1947 and again in 1954. Each time, in his view, he was cheated at the negotiating table of the gains he thought he had made in the battlefield. He no doubt feels, like Will Rogers, that he has won every war and lost every conference.

Nor, indeed, have we offered terms which are likely to strike the other side as anything more than a means of legitimatizing not just their defeat on the battlefield but the permanent eradication of the Viet Cong as any sort of political force in post-war South Vietnam. As we question Hanoi's readiness to negotiate, we must

[1] The proposal of a cease-fire on the ground in South Vietnam is very different and possibly very dangerous. Such a cease-fire should come at the end, not at the beginning, of negotiations.

also candidly question our own. For all our official statements about our willingness to go anywhere, talk to anyone, etc., it can hardly be said that the administration has pursued negotiation with a fraction of the zeal, imagination and perseverance with which it has pursued the war.

It cannot be said, for example, that the administration has laid fairly before the American people the occasional signals, however faint, which have come from Hanoi, as in the early winter of 1965-66, when U Thant's mediation reached the point of selecting the hotel in Rangoon where talks might take place, until we killed the idea by beginning the bombing of the north. Instead, we have repeatedly denied the existence of any peace feelers at all. When President Johnson said on October 6, 1966, "We pursue every indication that we have that might offer any possibilities, we always have an open mind, we're very anxious to find any basis for negotiation," his international audience could only gasp with incredulity. Nor, for all our declarations about "unconditional" negotiations, have we for one minute refrained from setting conditions—such as, for example, that we won't talk to the Viet Cong unless they come to the conference table disguised as North Vietnamese. Though we appear to have receded from this doctrine to the position that Viet Cong representation would not be an "insurmountable problem," our policy remains so equivocal that, given the Viet Cong's automatic mistrust of the discordant voices coming out of Washington, one can understand their impression that they have been given little solid reason to think that we mean to negotiate about anything except their unconditional surrender.

It is not hard to understand, for example, why our Manila proposal that we will remove our forces "not later than six months" after the other side pulls out of South Vietnam failed to move Hanoi deeply. If Hanoi had made the identical offer to us—that they would promise to withdraw six months after we did—we would hardly rush to embrace this as a serious proposition. Moreover, we have given several different impressions of what we mean when we ask Hanoi to withdraw "its forces" to the north. Ambassador Goldberg on September 22, 1966, spoke of the withdrawal of "all external forces—those of North Vietnam as well as those from the United States." On October 12 the Secretary of State said, "We shall leave when those invaders and arms from the North go home"; as for the "indigenous element . . . we consider it well within the capacity of the South Vietnamese to handle." But then on October 24 the Defense Department said that the conditions included "the intent that Viet Cong military units would be deactivated in any proposed withdrawal of external forces." At Manila we had spoken of withdrawing after the level of violence "subsides"; but on November 4, President Johnson, unilaterally amending the Manila offer, said that American troop withdrawal would not take place till six months after violence "ceases"—which evidently means until not only the North Vietnamese regulars withdraw but the South Vietnamese rebels give up: back again to unconditional surrender.

The future of the Viet Cong is, of course, central to negotiations, since they constitute the great bulk of the enemy in the field. But the American position here could hardly be more obscure. On the one hand, Vice President Humphrey has said that the fox should not be put into the chicken coop. On the other, Ambassador Goldberg has told the United Nations that the United States does not seek "to exclude any segment of the South Vietnamese people from peaceful participation in their country's future." "Allowing the Communists to help govern Vietnam," former Vice President Nixon has observed, "cannot be squared with the President's stated policy of no reward for aggression." But denying them a role in a government produced by free elections cannot be squared with the President's stated commitment: "We fight for the principle of self-determination that the people of South Vietnam should be able to choose their own course."

It is hard to see why we should not follow the precedent of Laos, when we admitted the Pathet Lao to the peace talks. Unless we mean to exterminate the Viet Cong, village by village, thicket by thicket, cave by cave, man by man, we must surely offer them the prospect of a say in the future political life of South Vietnam— conditioned on their laying down their arms, opening up their territories and abiding by the ground rules of free elections. Nor is there reason to see why we have been so reluctant again to follow the Geneva Agreements and the Laos model and loudly declare neutralization under international guarantee our long-run objective for Vietnam. An imaginative diplomacy would long since have discussed the ways and means of achieving such neutralization with Russia, France, Britain and other interested countries.[2]

Does this all imply a judgment that the Viet Cong could repent and become a housebroken, democratic party in a neutralized state? Not necessarily, any more than the inclusion of the Pathet Lao in a coalition government implied such a judgment in Laos. Yet, unless we mean to exterminate the Viet Cong, we must seek terms to which their future political behavior can be held. If negotiations should lead to a provisional regime charged with the responsibility of preparing for elections, and if the Viet Cong should be given representation in that regime (and no group could be expected to take part in elections prepared exclusively by their enemies), then we should not reject that process; and, if elections should lead to a coalition government, it should be noted that coalition may well have a different significance in Vietnam from what it would have in a western party system. As Professor H. J. Spiro has pointed out, in traditional oriental society "order was

[2] Lord Avon makes valuable suggestions to this end in *Toward Peace in Indochina* (Boston, 1966).

maintained or restored by consensual rather than oppositional procedures. . . . Attempts to engage in [consensus-restoring] negotiations would surprise many Americans, but they would seem quite natural in the oriental context."

One cannot exclude the possibility that "consensual" procedures might work and reintegrate the Viet Cong into the national life of South Vietnam. As Hanoi unquestionably has its own objectives independent of Peking, so the Viet Cong may well have their own objectives independent of Hanoi. Their insistence in the *maquis* has been that they want a free South Vietnam, not a unified Vietnam under Ho Chi Minh. Even though this may be propaganda, it may also express a tension between the Viet Cong and Hanoi, a tension which in the age of polycentrist communism could help protect the independence of a post-war South Vietnam.

Denis Warner, an experienced correspondent, deeply mistrustful of Vietnamese communism, discerned in November 1966 the possibility of "an exploitable split in the Vietcong ranks." He added, "The early tendency to dismiss the Front as a wholly Communist organization is being reviewed." Conceivably, he suggests, the southerners on both sides might in the end discover they have more in common with each other than with the northerners to whom they are presently allied.

Yet other scholars—Paul Mus, for example—detect an absolutism in Vietnamese politics which rejects compromise and consensus. Still, even if the Viet Cong should prove no more capable of collaboration with democratic parties than the Pathet Lao showed themselves in Laos in 1962-1963, the experiment in coalition plus neutralization might still have its uses, as it did in Laos. There the coalition formula, by offering the Pathet Lao representation in the government, induced them for a moment to stop fighting. At the same time, it separated the honest nationalists from the disciplined Communists within the Pathet Lao, and it gave Souvanna Phouma and the neutralists the genuine neutrality of their country to defend. When the Pathet Lao, failing to take over the government from within, withdrew from the coalition and resumed the civil war, this broke their old alliance with the neutralists, and Souvanna Phouma now moved to defend Laotian neutrality not against the United States but against communism. As a result, the coalition experiment shifted the balance of forces in Laos very much against the Pathet Lao. Unsatisfactory as the situation may be there today, it is still incomparably better than the situation in South Vietnam. At least no American soldiers are dying in Laos.

One cannot, of course, expect crystalline clarity on all possible issues before a negotiation begins; we cannot lay all our cards face up on the table before the talks start. Yet we must lay down enough to persuade the other side that it is worthwhile to join the game. And we must also remember that excessive and gratuitous ambiguity will strengthen doubts about American credibility (since ideologists, of whatever faith, will always attribute contradictory or shifting positions to machiavellian intention rather than to bureaucratic stupidity)—and that it may be doing so at a time when the world has other reasons to wonder about the fixity of our negotiating purpose. For we, like they, are trapped in the classic dilemma of negotiation: we do not want to negotiate when we are behind, because the other side will hold the better cards; but we do not want to negotiate when ahead either, because, if we wait a little longer, we will be still farther ahead and can demand even better terms. Americans seem especially vulnerable to fits of military optimism. Some American officials, moreover, unquestionably fear a negotiated settlement because they doubt the capacity of any foreseeable government in Saigon to deal with a Viet Cong resurgence after the departure of American troops. Whether they admit to themselves that the alternative is an indefinite American occupation of Vietnam, I do not know, but that is what the alternative is. One feels at times that nothing would cause greater consternation in certain offices in Washington than a decision in Hanoi to go to the conference table. Indeed, American scholars who have studied the matter believe that on a number of occasions when pressure for negotiation was mounting, we have, for whatever reason, stepped up the war.[3]

On the other hand, negotiation is not an exclusive, or even primary, American responsibility. Along with a military stalemate, the other precondition of a diplomatic settlement is surely a civilian government in Saigon. The military junta headed by Marshal Ky represents almost a new class of *nouveaux* mandarins. "They are the Vietnamese," Neil Sheehan has written, "who combine the worst of two cultures—the pretentiousness of the native mandarins and the rigidity of the French colonial officers and administrators." They will "tell Americans what they think Americans want to hear"; they will promulgate land-reform and tax-reduction decrees to soothe American advisers; but "all of these measures have been sabotaged because the regimes were and are composed of men who are members of, or are allied with, mandarin families that held title to properties they have no intention of renouncing. . . . They seek to retain what privileges they have and to regain those they have lost." Their regime is pervaded by nepotism, corruption and cynicism.

Marshal Ky, moreover, has become one of those Frankenstein's monsters we delight in creating in our client countries, very much like the egregious General Phoumi Nosavan, who single-handedly blocked a settlement in Laos for two years. Like Phoumi, Ky evidently feels that Washington has committed itself irrevocably to him—and why should he not after the laying on of hands at Honolulu and Manila?—and that, whatever he

[3] See *The Politics of Escalation in Vietnam* by Franz Schurman, Peter Dale Scott and Reginald Zelnick of the University of California. Available in a Fawcett Premier edition.

does, we cannot afford to abandon him. Quite naturally, he takes advantage of his opportunities to get *us* to do what will serve *his* interests—which, in effect, means a determination by a Vietnamese politician to make American policy on Vietnam. Not only has he proposed the invasion of North Vietnam; but he has repeatedly proclaimed his opposition to the American pursuit of a peaceful settlement. "No negotiations with communists; never," Ky cried on his return to Saigon after Manila. ". . . We will fight to the end. . . . We don't want to meet with the Viet Cong. . . . A coalition with the communists means suicide." As for the Constituent Assembly, whose election in September 1966 excited such idealistic hopes in the United States, 'the impression given by the junta," wrote R. W. Apple, Jr., in the *New York Times* (November 24, 1966) of Marshal Ky's attitude toward this valiant try at self-government, "has been one of disregard verging on contempt."

One cannot blame Ky for pursuing his own policies: one can only blame the American government for letting him try to decide American policy. And indulgence is naturally construed as complicity. Robert Shaplen reported to *The New Yorker* in August 1966 that the atmosphere there "is being compared to the miasma that surrounded Diem and his tyrannical brother Ngo Dinh Nhu" and that "many Vietnamese believe that the Americans, having embraced Ky so wholeheartedly and supported him so long, are just as responsible as his Government for the recent repressive acts." I am sure that President Johnson did not intend to turn over American policy and honor in Vietnam to Marshal Ky's gimcrack, bullyboy, get-rich-quick regime. The time is bound to come when Ky must learn the facts of life, as General Phoumi eventually and painfully learned them.

But why wait? In our whole time in Vietnam, there has never been a government in Saigon which had the active loyalty of the peasants; indeed, in the past, when the Saigon government has recovered control of territory from the Viet Cong, its first camp-followers have often been stooges of the oligarchy collecting back rents and taxes. It might be a useful experiment to encourage a pro-peasant regime to come into existence. Only a government which enlists enthusiastic popular support in the countryside—i.e., a government not dominated by the landlords—would stand any chance of dealing with a guerrilla resurgence, even should the North Vietnam forces be withdrawn. "What South Vietnam needs," President Marcos of the Philippines has said, "is the will to fight, which cannot be exported." Instead of identifying American interests with Ky and rebuffing the broader political impulses in South Vietnam, we should long since have welcomed a movement toward a civilian government representing the significant political forces of the country and capable both of rallying the army and carrying forward programs of social reform. We should give such a government all possible assistance in rebuilding and modernizing the political and institutional structures of South Vietnam. We should encourage it to take the lead in the political and diplomatic steps necessary to stop the war. If it should favor the neutralization of its country, if it should seek negotiation with the Viet Cong, even if it should release us from our commitment to stay in Vietnam, we should not therefore think that the world is coming to an end.

Of course we cannot now see the shape of a successful negotiation: all we can do is to define its limits. For one can rarely forecast the details of a political settlement. If we widen the war, we contract the possibilities for negotiation. If we slow the war down, we may open up possibilities which we cannot presently envisage. If we have learned anything from recent experience, it is surely the difficulty of predicting the resolution of crises in advance, from the blockade of Berlin to the nuclearization of Cuba. At each point, those who could not see how the crisis could logically be resolved pressed for drastic solutions; while those who understood the unpredictability of history insisted on avoiding irreversible actions. Our need now is to create a new situation—and then to take advantage of new opportunities. This means abandoning the policy of escalation, the policy which maximizes risks without producing results. This means above all that we must oppose further widening of the war.

It is not too late to begin the de-escalation of the war; nor would the reduction of our military effort damage our international influence. "There is more respect to be won in the opinion of this world," George Kennan has written, "by a resolute and courageous liquidation of unsound positions than by the most stubborn pursuit of extravagant or unpromising objectives." If our credibility is the issue, it is rather more important that other countries believe in our intelligence and responsibility than our passion for overkill. France was stronger than even after De Gaulle left Algeria, the Soviet Union suffered no lasting damage from pulling its nuclear missiles out of Cuba. And the policy of de-escalation recommended here is, of course, something a good deal less than withdrawal.

De-escalation *could* work, *if* there were the will to pursue it . . . This is the hard question. The administration, disposed to the indiscriminate use of power, enmeshed in the grinding cogs of the escalation machine, committed to the thesis that China is the enemy in Vietnam, obviously could not turn to de-escalation without considerable inner upheaval. The issue in the United States in the months to come will be whether President Johnson's leadership is sufficiently resilient and forbearing to permit a change in the direction of policy and arrest what is coming increasingly to seem an accelerating drift toward a great and unnecessary catastrophe.

IX

VIETNAM AND AMERICAN DEMOCRACY

*W*E FACE, in short, a test of our democracy. We must not let the war in Vietnam poison our national life, as Korea did briefly in the early fifties, or as Algeria poisoned France in the early sixties. We have an opportunity to prove our national maturity and show that we can undertake a major effort abroad, as we did during the Second World War, without wallowing in hysteria at home.

What are the chances of preserving our national poise this time? There are unfavorable as well as favorable factors in our present situation as compared with that fifteen years ago. For one thing, the intensity of the national administration's commitment to the Bill of Rights can make a vital difference. The reason why the Second World War (with a few exceptions, like the internment of the Japanese-Americans) was comparatively unstained by assaults on civil freedom was the libertarianism of Franklin Roosevelt and his administration. Similarly McCarthyism was more or less contained during the Truman years. It broke out of control only when the Eisenhower administration brought an attitude of indifference in the White House and of positive collaboration with McCarthy (Secretary of State Dulles, for example) down the line. Today, while President Johnson has manfully spoken up for the right to dissent on a number of occasions, one cannot be sure to what extent his heart is always in it. There were strange notes in his Honolulu attack on critics of his Vietnam policy as "callous or timid . . . blind to experience and deaf to hope," as well as in his Chicago outburst about "nervous Nellies" who break ranks "under the strain" and turn "on their leaders, their country and their own fighting men." It is hardly prudent for any President to insist on a conception of unity which, on closer examination, means no more than unquestioning acceptance of government policy. There seems merit to the suggestion of Clayton Fritchey, who ran public affairs at the Pentagon under General Marshall in the early days of the Korean War: "President Johnson and his official family are all in favor of freedom of speech—they are only against the exercise of it."

Moreover, the Joint Chiefs of Staff fifteen years ago unanimously opposed the escalation of the Korean War and thereby had a calming effect on national opinion, especially in the angry days after the recall of General MacArthur. But today the Joint Chiefs seem just as unanimously in favor of the escalation of the Vietnamese war, with all that implies. And the State Department, which strove last time for rationality in debate, is this time actively implying that criticism of the war should stop because it cheers up Ho Chi Minh. Criticism of a war always cheers up the enemy; but I do not recall that any government official admonished Abraham Lincoln to stop criticizing the Mexican war on the ground that it gave aid and comfort to Santa Anna.

Another difference between 1951 and 1967 is that then the liberal and intellectual community was united in the determination to maintain rational discussion. Today some of its members seem to be vying with the reactionaries in advancing the cause of political irrationality. This is, above all, a self-defeating tactic for intellectuals; for, if it becomes a competition in demagoguery and hysteria, the anti-intellectuals will always win. One hates to see intellectuals and liberals preparing the way for a new McCarthyism by debasing the level of public discussion and substituting stereotypes for sense and rage for reason.

These explosions of political irrationality, whether on the right or on the left, have a number of things in common. For one thing, both tend to express what has been an ancient national weakness—that is, a susceptibility to the conspiratorial interpretation of history. We have always fallen too easily for the notion that complex historical developments are the result of the machinations of little groups of nasty men. This is what Richard Hofstadter has called "the paranoid style in American politics." From the clamor against the Society of the Cincinnati and the Masons to contemporary conspiratorial fantasies, whether of the John Birch Society or of the devotees of the "power elite," whether of the followers of Robert Welch or those of C. Wright Mills, conspiracy has been a familiar theme in our political discourse.

It expresses itself today in the notion on the right that the Communists are fomenting the anti-war demonstrations in the United States, not to mention the Buddhist protests in Saigon and Hue, as well as in the theory, cherished, alas, in very high places in our government, that what we face in Southeast Asia is a premeditated system of Chinese aggression, organized in Peking, for which the Viet Cong in South Vietnam are merely the pretext and the spearhead. And it expresses itself in the notion on the left that our Vietnam policy is dictated by capitalists seeking to expand profits and markets or by generals plotting a preventive war against China. Both sides refuse to see history as it really is—an untidy and unkempt process, in which decisions are taken, not according to master plans, but in darkling confusion and obscurity, and where ignorance, accident, chance and stupidity play a larger role than machiavellian calculation.

The explosions of political irrationality have another feature in common: the function in each case is more to provide internal psychic satisfaction than to advance the cause in whose name they take place—more to ventilate emotions than to influence events. Refusing a man a seat in the Georgia legislature or a grave in Arlington brings us no closer to victory in Southeast Asia than mobbing a Secretary of Defense or burning a draft card deters a President from dropping napalm bombs. The serious restraint on the movement toward a wider war has been mostly the result of the coverage and force of individuals, whether in the United States Senate or in local meetings or community teach-ins, who, acting out of a thoughtful analysis of the drift of our policy, have succeeded in bringing into existence a serious debate on our choice in the Far East. It has come, not from the outpouring of emotion, but from the application of reason.

Yet, if we have certain disadvantages today in comparison with fifteen years ago, we also have certain advantages—most notably the memory of the earlier experience. McCarthyism gave the country a kind of inoculation, and the immunity has not yet worn off, as the voters of New Jersey showed in November 1965 in rejecting the effort to make Professor Genovese's views on Vietnam the central issue of the gubernatorial campaign. A number of national figures, recalling the excesses of fifteen years ago, are showing an admirable determination to prevent a repeat performance.

These figures are not to be found in the United States where they would be found in England—that is, in the so-called Establishment. It has become recently fashionable to denounce the arrogance of the American Establishment. But one sometimes wonders whether the trouble with the American Establishment has been so much its arrogance as its cowardice—in other words, its fear of acting as an Establishment should. The point of an Establishment, I take it, is to provide support for the established values and institutions of society. This has been the triumph of the original Establishment in Great Britain. It is impossible to imagine a McCarthy terrorizing British public life: the Establishment would never permit it.

But the so-called American Establishment crumpled up before McCarthy. The great leaders of American business and the bar said hardly a word in protest. One eminent figure—whom Establishment scholars have thought to be the chairman of the American Establishment at the time—actually suggested in a public speech that the inquiries of the McCarthy committee were no worse than Senator Black's investigations into the public utility holding companies in 1935. No doubt such leaders of respectable opinion became anti-McCarthy once the crisis was over; but, whatever the retrospective courage, let us avoid the illusion that the American Establishment will be much braver the next time round. The nation will have to look to stouter and more principled figures if it is to contain another epidemic of political panic.

One place to look, I think, will be in Washington itself. Responsible men in public life recognize the damage that a new outbreak of national hysteria will do both to our own sense of purpose and to the world's confidence in our leadership. Thus Secretary McNamara in a recent speech pointedly quoted Judge Learned Hand's eloquent statement in the midst of the McCarthy years: "I believe that community is already in process of dissolution where each man begins to eye his neighbor as a possible enemy, where nonconformity with the accepted creed, political as well as religious, is a mark of disaffection, where denunciation, without specification or backing, takes the place of evidence, where orthodoxy chokes freedom of dissent. . . . The mutual confidence on which all else depends can be maintained only by an open mind and a brave reliance upon free discussion." The Secretary of Defense then added on his own what seems a tacit rebuke of his over-zealous colleagues in the Johnson administration: "Whatever comfort some of the extremist protest may be giving our enemies—and it is clear from Hanoi's own statements that it is—let us be perfectly clear about our principles and our priorities. This is a nation in which the freedom of dissent is absolutely fundamental."

So Senator Fulbright has issued thoughtful warnings: "The longer the Vietnamese war goes on without prospect of victory or negotiated peace, the war fever will rise, hopes will give way to fears, and tolerance and freedom of discussion will give way to a false and strident patriotism." So the Executive Council of the American Federation of Teachers canceled the action of its Las Vegas local in expelling the teacher who refused to salute the flag in silent protest against the war in Vietnam. So Senator Edward M. Kennedy of Massachusetts protested to the State Department over the surveillance of the Harvard professor and brought this particular form of snooping to an end. So Senator Robert Kennedy of New York read aloud on the floor of the Senate an editorial from the *Washington Daily News* condemning the decision not to bury the Communist war hero in Arlington. "We learn from our mistakes," the editorial said "—and one of our lessons is that to hate and harry the sinner to his grave is hardly in the American tradition." Robert Kennedy was later heard to say somberly that he did not think anyone now buried in Arlington would object to the holder of the Distinguished Service Cross lying there, so he could not see why veterans' organizations were so agitated about it. So the Supreme Court has canceled the refusal of the Georgia legislature to seat a critic of the Vietnam war.

Leadership by public figures and the press offers one hope of preventing the revival of McCarthyism. And there is another favorable difference between the United States today and fifteen years ago—that is, the increased size and weight of the academic community. There are twice as many students enrolled in institutions of higher education in the country as there were a short decade ago. By the end of the sixties there will be almost three-quarters of a million teachers in our colleges and universities and seven million students. This amounts to a formidable political constituency—and one which can be counted on to be uncommonly bright, well informed, articulate and irascible. Indeed, the expansion of the academic community has already begun to affect the tone and character of our politics. It is hard to throw a stone on college campuses today without hitting a visiting politician.

The academic community will be, among other things, a constituency for the Bill of Rights. For, freedom of inquiry and dissent, if the general interest of the nation, is the class interest of the academic community. Of course, if the academic community is to strengthen the body politic against irrationality, it must clear itself of suspicion that irrationality is its own favorite form of expression. Students must have other models than Latin American universities and other ambitions than working for their L.S.D. And the faculty must stick by its professional faith in reasoned discourse and not give the impression that it regards slogan and emotion as the hot way to deal with complicated issues. Perhaps all this is too much to expect; and, in the end, the academic community, like the Establishment, will prove incapable of fighting intelligently for rational discussion.

But perhaps not. One is heartened by the way that college faculties, presidents and even boards of trustees and overseers are speaking up in defense of the Bill of Rights—and on occasions when the expression involved may have been a good deal less than rational. The New Jersey case a year ago was one notable example. In the spring of 1966 the president of the Indiana University defending the right of an undergraduate organization to invite a Communist to give a lecture, observed sensibly that "a closed campus is not a sound way to engender belief in an open society." The president of the board of trustees added, "We have strong faith in the intelligence of our students to separate fact from falsehood" and warned critics against having the university "deny the constitutional guarantee of freedom of speech in the anger and frustration of the world situation at this point in history."

I hope one is wrong in supposing that this anger and frustration, welling up as a result of the Vietnam involvement, may portend another crisis of our national freedom. But, if no such crisis comes, it will only be because individuals throughout the land take a clear and firm stand for sanity. "The men who create power," President Kennedy said a few weeks before he was murdered in Dallas in the supreme act of political irrationality in our time, "make an indispensable contribution to the nation's greatness, but the men who question power make a contribution just as indispensable." This is an exact statement of the oldest American tradition; and that tradition will live only as citizens speak out for freedom in their own communities and by their own firesides. In retrospect, we have always regretted our spasms of repression and persecution; we have gained nothing from them—McCarthy never found a Communist—and have invariably hated ourselves in the morning. Why would a nation, billing itself as the "land of the free" and aspiring to the leadership of mankind, once again parade its hypocrisies, surrender to its fears, defile its oldest ideals and disgrace itself in the eyes of the world and its own posterity?

For whatever the outcome of the Vietnam debate or of later debates that may darken our future, the essential thing is to preserve mutual trust among ourselves as Americans. Let us remember that those who take a different position—whether they want to evacuate Saigon or bomb Hanoi—may also be actuated by honorable and patriotic motives—may, whatever their degree of error, still have a genuine concern for peace and freedom. Let us always distinguish between disagreement and disloyalty, between opposition and treason. Let us never forget that complicated problems can be resolved only by reasoned analysis; and that the insistence on reason is the final hope of democratic society. If we can remember this, in whatever direction our decisions and destiny take us, we can preserve and cherish our fundamental unity of purpose as Americans.